Teach Reading, Not Testing

Teach Reading, Not Testing

Best Practice in an Age of Accountability

Liz Hollingworth ▪ Hilleary M. Drake

Foreword by W. James Popham

CORWIN
A SAGE Company

CORWIN
A SAGE Company

FOR INFORMATION:

Corwin
A SAGE Company
2455 Teller Road
Thousand Oaks, California 91320
(800) 233-9936
Fax: (800) 417-2466
www.corwin.com

SAGE Ltd.
1 Oliver's Yard
55 City Road
London EC1Y 1SP
United Kingdom

SAGE Pvt. Ltd.
B 1/I 1 Mohan Cooperative Industrial Area
Mathura Road, New Delhi 110 044
India

SAGE Asia-Pacific Pte. Ltd.
33 Pekin Street #02-01
Far East Square
Singapore 048763

Acquisitions Editor: Carol Chambers Collins
Associate Editor: Megan Bedell
Editorial Assistant: Sarah Bartlett
Project Editor: Veronica Stapleton
Copy Editor: Janet Ford
Typesetter: C&M Digitals (P) Ltd.
Proofreader: Dennis W. Webb
Indexer: Terri Corry
Cover Designer: Scott Van Atta
Permissions Editor: Adele Hutchinson

Printed in the United States of America

Library of Congress Cataloging-in-Publication Data

Hollingworth, Liz.

Teach reading, not testing : best practice in an age of accountability/Liz Hollingworth and Hilleary M. Drake ; foreword by W. James Popham.

p. cm.
Includes bibliographical references and index.

ISBN 978-1-4129-9773-7 (pbk.)

1. Reading (Elementary) 2. Motivation in education. I. Drake, Hilleary M. II. Title.

LB1573.H4622 2012
372.4—dc23   2011039001

This book is printed on acid-free paper.

11 12 13 14 15 10 9 8 7 6 5 4 3 2 1

Contents

Foreword

Teachers' Pets or Teachers' Frets?

Educational Tests: Are they teachers' *pets* or, these days, are they teachers' *frets*? Putting it more prosaically, should today's teachers regard tests as the friends or enemies of their instruction efforts? This seemingly simple question, more potent than it first appears, requires a far-from-simple answer. Yet, providing a practical answer to the pet/fret puzzle is the central premise of an exciting new book about reading instruction by Liz Hollingworth and Hilleary Drake. Honestly, who could imagine a more propitious moment for a book about the teaching and the testing of reading to rumble onto our educational stage?

Let's face it, when it comes to the way most teachers currently view externally imposed educational tests, this could surely be characterized as "the worst of times." Most teachers view large-scale educational tests—particularly those tests linked to federal or state accountability programs—as downright nuisances or worse. There's not the slightest hint that today's test-dominated schooling somehow can also be regarded as "the best of times."

Droves of teachers now regard accountability tests as a bona fide blight on their educational landscapes. Externally imposed, most high-stakes exams are seen to constrain the curriculum, transform teaching into test-preparation, and remove much of the genuine joy that should be found in our classrooms. No, today's accountability tests do not rank high on most teachers' popularity parades.

It is against this pervasive, profoundly negative backdrop that Hollingworth and Drake have set out to suggest how externally imposed accountability tests could have a positive impact on elementary teachers' reading instruction. These two authors have, clearly, chosen a potentially sour cherry on which to chew. But, as will become clear while reading the Hollingworth-Drake book, there are magic classroom moments when, if teachers truly understand what's going on with the external tests being used, results of those tests can spur a teacher to adopt the sorts of instructional choices likely to benefit students.

At first glance, this seems to be a book about how to teach reading. But a closer look will reveal that it's a book about how to teach reading while dodging the adverse impact of inappropriate large-scale testing. Indeed, the book is peppered with suggestions about how to pick up positive payoffs from typical standardized reading tests. It's a book, in short, about how to use external tests as effectively as possible to enhance students' reading skills.

In the book's early pages, the authors tell us they want their book to (1) provide teaching tips for elementary reading classrooms, (2) ensure that all students are prepared for high-stakes reading tests, and (3) show teachers how to supply such test-preparation without "teaching to a test." Those are three laudable aspirations. But you'll also see another significant theme slithering in and out of the book's chapters. Hollingworth and Drake, you see, want young children to *love* reading.

That's right, these authors recognize not only the *necessity* for today's students to read—in school and once school is over—but also the immense *pleasure* that reading can bring to anyone who reads with reasonable comprehension. The book frequently reminds teachers how important it is to have students *enjoy* the act of reading. Whether children are reading a hardback book, a laptop computer screen, or the words wafted to them by tomorrow's next-generation electronic device—reading should gratify the reader. And, regrettably, readers' gratification cannot be taken for granted. It, as with many covert variables, needs to be assessed.

Perhaps, if we put as much assessment energy into measuring students' attitudes toward reading as we put into measuring students' ability to spot a paragraph's main idea, we'd stimulate more teachers to engender positive reading attitudes along with higher test scores. We do, in truth, measure what we treasure. But if we only yammer about getting students to groove on reading, and never get around to actually assessing students' attitudes toward reading, then we send a strikingly clear message that students' attitudes toward reading really aren't important.

Hollingworth and Drake make a sincere effort to strip away the mystery from how large-scale reading tests are born. What few teachers recognize is that the most fundamental steps in the creation of an accountability test in reading are not remarkably different from what takes place when a teacher creates a classroom test of reading. Although reading tests typically emerge from big-box measurement companies—often behind closed doors—there's little going on when high-stakes reading tests are built that's incomprehensible to most teachers.

This new book is loaded with practical suggestions regarding how elementary teachers can do a niftier job with their reading instruction. Of particular merit is the authors' early-on treatment of alignment. This is because their analysis of the necessary match among curricular aims, classroom instructional activities, and high-stakes achievement tests sets the stage for their subsequent recommendations regarding how to avoid "teaching to the test." Indeed, one of the book's continuing themes revolves around how teachers can help students score well on externally required accountability tests without those teachers' turning their classrooms into test-preparation factories.

Co-authored books often feature a pair of collaborating professors or, perhaps, two in-the-trenches teachers. In this book, however, we encounter a delightful blend of one university academic and one K–12 classroom teacher. It is clear that the assessment and instructional views of these two friends has, on occasion, been sharpened by the career experiences of their co-author. The result is a readable account of how teachers of reading can go about their work in a way that external tests can become, if not a flat-out friends, at least not lasting enemies.

W. James Popham
Emeritus Professor
University of California, Los Angeles

Acknowledgments

Liz and Hilleary met in August 2002 in a graduate class on Educational Measurement and Evaluation at the University of Iowa, just as the No Child Left Behind Act was becoming law. In that class, we sat alongside teachers, school counselors, and future psychometricians to learn about the promises and limitations of testing.

Since then, as reading teachers, we have watched with wonder and dismay as our colleagues have struggled with the pressures of the accountability movement.

This book is written using stories from both of our classrooms. We know for sure that standardized reading tests are designed to measure a student's ability to read. What confuses us is how educators confuse test preparation with content knowledge. We hope this book helps reading teachers sort through the differences.

The idea for this book stems from an article by Liz that was published in *The Reading Teacher* (Hollingworth, 2007), titled "Five Ways to Prepare for Standardized Tests Without Sacrificing Best Practice." For the success of that article, we thank our friend and colleague, Janet Smith, a writing teacher for at-risk high schoolers and an excellent test editor.

We have Liz's daughter, Emily, to thank for the illustrations that appear in Chapters 1 and 2.

Thank you to the fifth graders at Rendezvous Elementary in Riverton, Wyoming, for helping us think through some of our ideas from a kid-perspective.

A big thank you to Jim Stachowiak in the Iowa Center for Assistive Technology Education and Research (ICATER) lab for reading an early draft of Chapter 6, and for teaching the University of Iowa students every semester about the newest technologies to accommodate students with special needs.

We would also like to thank our colleagues at Iowa Testing Programs for welcoming us both into the educational measurement and statistics community, despite our literacy backgrounds and aversion to statistics and graphing calculators. We especially appreciate the coaching from

Professor Timothy Ansley, Director of the *Iowa Tests of Educational Development*, who likes to joke at inservices with teachers that he's starting to feel like test development has become the *Dark Side of the Force*. Thank you to Dr. Gayle Babbitt Bray, Senior Reading Editor for the *Iowa Tests of Basic Skills*, for teaching us how to craft elegant reading tests.

Despite the help from friends and colleagues, the ideas and opinions expressed in this book are ours alone and should not be interpreted as any official statement or position of Iowa Testing Programs or the University of Iowa.

Liz would like to dedicate this book to the late Professor Albert N. Hieronymus, friend and former Director of the *Iowa Basic Skills Testing Program* from 1948 to 1987. Having been a classroom teacher himself, Al understood the value and importance of teachers (considering he met his wife when they were teaching together, and that several of his children and grandchildren grew up to be teachers and professors), and he envisioned the Iowa tests first and foremost as a tool to help teachers better meet the needs of their students. Al is a role model for the ways faculty in a college of education can impact public schools in a positive way through their research, teaching, and service.

Hilleary would like to dedicate this book to Mrs. Donna Kuhlman, her eighth-grade English teacher at Canyon Junior High School. Mrs. Kuhlman saw early on in the testing craze in Texas in the early 1990s that she needed to protect her curriculum, her instructional time, and her students from the frenzy of test preparation. She was a motivating, challenging, and inspiring educator who refused to succumb to the pressures of test preparation. She knew that her students deserved and were capable of so much more than just the minimum to *pass the test*. Thank you Mrs. Kuhlman, as both a student and now a teacher, for believing there was no better test preparation than fabulous teaching. You were (and still are!) so right.

PUBLISHER'S ACKNOWLEDGMENTS

Corwin gratefully acknowledges the contributions of the following reviewers:

Kelly Aeppli-Campbell, K–12 Reading Supervisor
Escambia County School District
Escambia, FL

Norma Barber, English Teacher
Ukiah School District 80R
Ukiah, OR

Janice C. Brunson, Elementary Literacy Coordinator
Stafford County Public Schools
Stafford, VA

Lorenza Lara, Secondary Literacy Coordinator
Department of Teaching and Learning
Denver Public Schools
Denver, CO 80203

Paula J. Leftwich, Senior Director, K–12 Curriculum and Instruction
School District of Polk County
Jim Miles Professional Development Center
Lakeland, FL

Sandy Moore, English Teacher
Coupeville High School
Coupeville, WA

Kay Teehan, Literacy Coach/Media Specialist
Bartow Middle School
Bartow, FL

Kristina Turner, English Teacher
T.L. Hanna High School
Anderson, SC

Robert H. Williams, Jr., Associate Professor of English
Editor, *Virginia English Bulletin*
Radford University
Radford, VA

About the Authors

 **Liz Hollingworth** (right) is a professor in the College of Education at the University of Iowa. Her research and teaching interests are centered on curriculum, leadership, and assessment. In particular, her work explores how federal school reform policies affect classroom practice. Her other books include *Organization and Administration of Iowa Public and Private Schools* and *Complicated Conversations: Race and Ideology in an Elementary Classroom*. Dr. Hollingworth grew up in San Diego, taught in Chicago and Michigan, and now lives in Iowa City with her husband, Andrew, and teenage daughter, Emily.

Hilleary M. Drake (left) has taught fifth grade for six years in Riverton, Wyoming. Growing up in Texas during the initial wave of the "testing craze," she understands just how harmful it can be when testing drives instruction. She earned her undergraduate degree from Texas A&M–Corpus Christi and her master's degree from the University of Iowa. While at Iowa she worked with Iowa Testing Progams as a graduate assistant, gaining behind-the-scene knowledge of the testing industry. Hilleary enjoys reading, traveling, and spending time with friends and family, especially her husband, Jay.

Introduction

Since the passage of No Child Left Behind legislation in 2001 (NCLB), we have worked with teams of teachers and school administrators, discussing test items, negotiating student performance level descriptors, and, ultimately, setting **cut scores** for **accountability** purposes with personnel from state departments of education. We both have also been lucky enough to work with a state department of education as it develops a comprehensive system of accountability that includes standards for teaching, learning, and classroom formative **assessment.**

As we go about this work, we are troubled by what the teachers in the front lines tell us about how students are being prepared for test taking in this era of accountability. Many educators report feeling compelled to abandon what they know to be the best ways to teach reading in exchange for a test-preparation curriculum designed to raise test scores. Other schools have hired independent consulting firms, staffed by well-meaning, smart people who nevertheless have no classroom experience or educational background, to coach veteran teachers on how to teach test-taking strategies to increase reading scores. Why are educators so ready to turn over their professional voices and expertise?

The atmosphere the NCLB created in classrooms across the United States can explain this sudden lack of confidence. Many teachers find themselves judged by the test scores of their students—test scores that are affected by factors beyond their control: students' academic history, students' abilities, school facilities and equipment, transience of the population, socioeconomic class, and so on. It is not surprising that teachers who are threatened with pay for performance incentives or reorganization based on the student body's **adequate yearly progress (AYP)** would feel compelled to change how they teach for the promise of improved test scores, even if it means giving up strategies for teaching reading and writing that research and experience show are effective. What can teachers do in the classroom to help students prepare for a high-stakes, standardized, multiple-choice reading test without sacrificing what they know to be best practice?

This book is designed to give reading teachers practical tools to improve reading test scores without forgetting everything we've learned about the best ways to teach kids how to be literate and how to *love* reading. This is particularly important in light of the pressures to raise student test scores in reading in this age of accountability.

Our intention with this book is threefold:

1. to provide teaching tips to use in an elementary reading classroom,

2. to make sure that *all* students are prepared for the high-stakes reading tests, without causing more work for teachers, and

3. to accomplish this preparation without teaching to the test.

For some readers who have worked in elementary schools a long time, the policy background or the teaching techniques may not be new. We expect these readers to find this book a useful tool to use in professional development inservices, particularly Chapter 6. For educators charged with purchasing technology to support reading initiatives in schools, we believe Chapter 3 will be particularly helpful to you. For elementary principals who are looking for ethical strategies to raise building reading test scores without asking teachers to use skill-and-drill-worksheets, this book is for you!

NCLB has caused a myriad of unintended consequences for literacy educators, especially in schools in danger of not meeting AYP. An overemphasis on teaching the portions of the reading domain that are testable with large-scale assessments, like spelling and finding facts from a reading passage, narrows the language arts curriculum in ways that go against what teachers know is the best way to teach. For example, in order to target reading instruction at students at varying developmental levels, some schools have adopted reading curricula that limit the choices for children's literature if the books are not on a reading level that has been determined by a publishing company to be academically appropriate. Adult readers don't chose books that way, so why should we train our children that books must be challenging to be worth reading? Students don't develop a lifelong love of reading without practicing reading what interests them.

As educators, we must hold our ground as professionals and refuse to compromise our excellent tried and true teaching practices in the name of higher test scores. The tests themselves are not the problem; in fact, the test scores can provide teachers with valuable information about student performance on basic language arts skills. But, teaching only the skills that can be tested leads to a narrowing of the curriculum and to the deprofessionalization of teachers. It is crucial that the expertise of teachers be brought to bear on curriculum decisions at the classroom level.

WHAT WE'VE LEARNED
ABOUT THE TESTING INDUSTRY

Liz and Hilleary met in 2002 in an educational measurement class at the University of Iowa. We both had graduate assistantships with Iowa Testing Programs researching and developing tests for the *Iowa Tests of Basic Skills* (ITBS). Amazingly, our first year at this new job was the year NCLB was passed.

What we know is that good readers should be able to use a number of strategies to approach a novel text. These strategies can be taught in school. Test preparation worksheets are boring, and they don't make kids better readers. In fact, really good reading tests are virtually impervious to test prep. That is, if a test taker is successful on the test, it is because he or she is a good reader, not because he or she is a good test taker.

In Ketter and Pool's (2001) article, *Exploring the impact of a high-stakes direct writing assessment in two high school classrooms*, the authors write that "critics of standardized multiple choice testing believe that teaching to such tests narrows the range of activities in which students engage" (p. 344). In many school districts, the stakes placed on test scores have created an academic environment where what is tested can affect what is taught, an idea that runs counter to best practice for **psychometricians** (test developers) and teachers alike.

It may surprise some teachers to hear this, but the testing industry as a whole does not claim that student learning can be assessed only with standardized tests. For example the *Iowa Tests Interpretive Guide for Teachers and Counselors* says "many of the common misuses [of the tests] stem from depending on the scores from a single test or test battery to make an important decision about a student or a class of students," (Hoover et al., 2003, p. 11). Certainly standardized, multiple-choice tests can be used to assess reading comprehension, spelling, and grammar, but when high stakes are placed on the tests, the consequences can be profound. It forces English teachers to spend class time focusing on a slice of what teachers want their students to be able to do, because the assessment of an English teacher's teaching and of student performance is based on the standardized tests of reading comprehension and language skills. The end result can be a crowding out of all the kinds of learning that English teachers believe are important in exchange for more reading comprehension, throwing the balance of the curriculum off.

Nothing can replace teacher observation, and a single test score should never be used to make an important decision about a student or a class of students, but there are some things that standardized tests *can* do extremely well. A good achievement battery can provide teachers achievement data on students' general reading comprehension skills that make it possible to monitor year-to-year developmental changes and can provide a basis for reports to parents that will enable home and school to work together in the students' best interests.

The standardized delivery of the assessment ensures fairness, and machine-scorable tests are an efficient and relatively inexpensive way to get a great deal of valuable information about student achievement in a short amount of time. Historically, however, when the stakes are high for teachers and students, there is a temptation for tests to drive the curriculum.

How Standardized Tests Are Made

One way to improve communication between teachers and test makers is to make visible the test development process. Many graduates of teacher education programs enter the classroom with limited understanding of test development for classroom use or of measurement concepts like norms and grade level equivalencies. When some light is shed on how standardized tests are made, perhaps teachers and curriculum experts can discover where there are opportunities to participate in the standardized test development in their districts.

Writing a standardized test requires some training to do it well. To build a reading test, test developers look for high quality, diverse literature, on a broad range of topics, written for children and young adults that has probably not been seen by the students before in order to ensure a level playing field for all test takers. The people engaged in this search are teachers, professors, graduate students working on degrees in educational measurement, and editors. We frequent garage sales and used book stores looking for books or articles on interesting topics, and we keep a massive database of every children's book that has won a major book award or has been excerpted in a textbook to avoid choosing a text that might privilege a group of students with prior experience with that text.

You should know that some test companies *"home brew"* their reading passages. What this means is that rather than find a piece of published text, they hire writers to create an original passage on a topic of their choice. For the test developers, that makes it easy to ensure that there is enough *meat* to the text to ask questions, and it guarantees that the topic will meet all of the requirements for the test specifications. For example, if the state requires 500-word nonfiction biographical sketch at eighth grade, a test developer can save time reading biographies written for eighth graders and culling the material to 500 interesting words by just writing something original. What is more, the topic can be easily state specific (think: Abraham Lincoln in Illinois or John Glenn in Ohio).

When a customized test for a particular state is built, the content standards are used as guides to write items that align with the curriculum. When we build a test battery for academic achievement, like the *Iowa Tests of Basic Skills* (Hoover, Dunbar, & Frisbie, 2001) and *Iowa Tests of Educational Development* (Forsyth, Ansley, Feldt, & Alnot, 2001), we write more general reading comprehension items that measure a student's ability to comprehend facts in the text, to make inferences, and to generalize from what they have read, skills that separate proficient readers from developing readers.

After we write and edit items (a process that frankly takes months of wordsmithing and involves dozens of item writers and editors), we field-test them, both statewide and nationally, at multiple grade levels in order to decide which items are best suited at each grade.

The data from those tryouts are analyzed item-by-item for **bias** on race, ethnicity, socioeconomic class, sex, geographical region, and private, Catholic, or public schools. Items where bias is detected are thrown out, and items that span a range of difficulty are selected. We also analyze the item response data for optimal functioning to see what percentage of students who scored high on the test as a whole got each item correct and to be sure that each item is functioning as we intend.

Once the reading tests have been piloted and the final items have been selected, we administer the tests around the country. The data from those administrations are used to build national norms so that teachers, parents, students, and other stakeholders can get a sense of how their students are reading compared to other children like them across the country. Our norms are available on the same categories that we use in our bias review: race, ethnicity, socioeconomic class, sex, geographical region, and private, Catholic, or public schools. So, for example, a school in a rural part of the country can have norms that show how their fourth-grade students performed on the ITBS reading test compared to all of the other students in rural schools nationally.

So What Good Are the Data From Standardized Tests?

The other important score that comes from the norming process is grade equivalents. When a seventh-grade student's ITBS Reading Comprehension score is compared with all of the other seventh graders who took the test in the fall of seventh grade, we can provide a report that says overall, your seventh grader performed on the test like most seventh graders in their third month of middle school. Now alone, this information probably isn't particularly interesting. But when a high school teacher looks at a student's cumulative school record and sees that every year this student scores at grade level, that teacher has some evidence of measured yearly growth and a picture of academic progress in reading over time begins to form. This information is by no means the only data that should be presented to parents wanting to know how their child's reading comprehension is progressing. However, norms and grade equivalents are a relatively inexpensive, time-efficient, and fair way of comparing student performance nationally, not just locally.

In short, the primary reason for using a standardized achievement battery is to gather information that can be used to help improve instruction. Standardized tests do not measure all the worthwhile outcomes of an English curriculum; the diversity of instructional methods and materials makes it impractical for any test to attempt to do that. However, there are a number of generally held outcomes toward which all students are expected to progress as they go through school, regardless of the specific courses they take or the curriculum they may be following. These skills, which cut across the curriculum and may be the province of more than one department, are among the major goals of literacy education.

CHAPTER OVERVIEWS

This book offers an approach to test preparation that does not require that teachers sacrifice everything they know about the best ways to teach kids to read. Test preparation worksheets and drill-and-kill activities do not make children into lifelong readers. Throughout the book, I provide research from the academic community to support the strategies and theories that are offered. In addition, I include stories from the field about the ways the accountability movement is corrupting teaching practice and what can be done about it.

Chapter 1 describes ways to be sure that what you are teaching in your classroom matches what is going to be tested. Alignment studies are an important way to ensure that you and your students are getting a more accurate picture from the test scores of what kids know and are able to do. This is not the same as teaching to the test, which is an incredibly important distinction.

Chapter 2 offers suggestions for the use of formative assessments in literacy contexts in order to check learning as you go. For the most part, any assessment can be used in a formative way, so don't be suckered in by merchants trying to sell you a magic Formative Test.

Chapter 3 is a conversation about teaching literacy with special populations. There is a helpful table of assistive technology devices that can be used in the service of teaching literacy to students with disabilities and with English language learners. In addition, a breakdown of the differences between accommodations and modifications is given, along with the history of policy and legislation that have guided best practice in special education in the United States.

Chapter 4 provides a discussion of motivation research to give teachers and administrators insight into why bribery (for example, pizza parties) doesn't have the kind of impact on test scores that one might expect. Some of the research I have conducted into ways schools try to motivate children on high-stakes tests is summarized in this chapter as well.

Chapter 5 gives an overview of ways we can connect reading units to real-world contexts to model for students what lifelong readers do. This chapter also provides suggestions for approaching test passages as a genre study in your classroom, including a conversation about how standardized, multiple-choice tests are developed.

Chapter 6 reviews best practice in teaching reading at the elementary level, including a conversation about theory and practice, and what to do when you feel that your expertise in teaching literacy is threatened by the reading programs being implemented in your district.

Chapter 7 concludes with implications for your teaching and with some advice for school leaders who are in a position to make a real difference with the policies they support.

END-OF-CHAPTER QUIZZES FOR DISCUSSION

A short vignette, followed by a quiz, appears at the end of each chapter to provide fertile ground for lively faculty discussions or book club-like conversations with your colleagues. We envision a book study group using these as the talking points to start their discussions at the beginnings of the meetings.

For some readers, the scenarios may seem wildly fictitious. Let me assure you that every one of the examples we give have come from practitioners who have described to me personally what has been happening in their schools. For those of you for whom the examples seem all too familiar, you have our sympathies and our support.

GLOSSARY

Be sure to look at the end of the book for a glossary of assessment terms. Hopefully it will serve as a resource for you as you read.

1 Conducting an Alignment Study

Chapter Highlights

- How to determine the alignment between the curriculum standards and what you teach by conducting an alignment study
- How to determine any areas missing from your curriculum by conducting a gap analysis
- How to supplement any missing areas to ensure all standards are being taught

Without question, teachers are faced with intense pressures to address the individual needs of students who come to their classrooms with a wide range of reading habits and abilities. This differentiation of instruction becomes even more difficult when reading groups are designated by an external literacy coordinator, mostly based on results from a district-selected reading test. There is also great pressure on teachers to address multiple facets of reading for all kids: fluency, vocabulary, phonics, decoding, and comprehension skills and strategies. And in this age of accountability, teacher quality is measured using student test scores.

The high-stakes reading tests hang like a cloud over our schools. Is it any wonder then that teachers devote so much class time to activities that promise to raise test scores? But before we scrap all of the research-based *best practices* in our tool kit in exchange for a test-preparation curriculum, consider this: if we know the best ways to teach students to read and the reading skills are aligned with what is being measured on the tests, the scores will take care of themselves.

Teaching reading is rocket science! Don't believe me? Take a stroll into any reading classroom today. Long gone are the days of the Bluebirds,

Redbirds, and Blackbirds; gone are the days where students are expected to work quietly and independently in pursuit of their deep, burning desire to be a good reader. OK, perhaps it was never quite that idyllic, but things have changed drastically in the elementary reading classroom over the last decade. Teachers now must address, for students at various levels, the multiple facets of reading, including fluency, vocabulary, phonics, decoding, and comprehension. This must be done, in many cases, from one central reading curriculum. And let's face it; most teachers have little say in choosing that program. As if all this weren't enough to cram into a reading block, let's not forget the pressures that come from outside sources, such as a literacy consultant or a reading coach. While well intentioned and well researched with their input, I don't know of many reading teachers who don't feel pressure from being pulled in one more direction as a coach makes suggestions for interventions for a student or group of students.

Sometimes it seems as if forces beyond our control have taken over the reading classroom. It's time to take back our reading programs. The best way to start is to take stock of your reading curriculum by conducting an **alignment** study.

CONDUCTING AN ALIGNMENT STUDY

The No Child Left Behind Act of 2001 (NCLB) is a continuation of a public policy in education that is grounded in the belief that school improvement can be achieved through the use of accountability measures and standards-based education. Standards-based education hinges on the idea that there is a set of written, curricular standards that describe expectations for student learning and achievement, and assessments are used to monitor achievement. Accountability policy assumes an aligned system, and alignment studies of content standards and test items are the key to demonstrating validity.

This chapter explains this *aligned* system and gives instructions on how to conduct your own alignment study to be certain that what you teach in your classroom is in line with what the state and district standards have outlined in the grade-level expectations. This stands in stark contrast with teaching to the test. Let's start with some definitions:

WHAT IS ALIGNMENT?

Alignment: Alignment can be reported as a matter of the degree to which a curriculum's scope and sequence matches a testing program's evaluation measures.

Similarly, alignment can refer to the degree to which a teacher's instruction matches the given curriculum.

Is what you're teaching what the standards dictate you teach?

Is what you're testing what you're teaching?

Imagine it as a pyramid (see Figure 1.1).

What this means is that if you are teaching a lesson on subject-verb agreement, it would be out of alignment to give the students a spelling test to see what they learned.

What you teach should end up being what you test (and not the other way around!).

You can conduct your own alignment study between the curriculum standards and your lesson plans to ensure everything that is expected in your state at each grade level is being taught. In short, an alignment study requires a team of curriculum experts to review the connection between the state standards that describe what should be taught and the school curriculum that describes what is actually taught, and match that against what is tested.

Don't panic if your school or district has not done this. It is not going to require you to hire a consultant to come in; as a teacher of this curriculum,

Figure 1.1 Alignment Pyramid

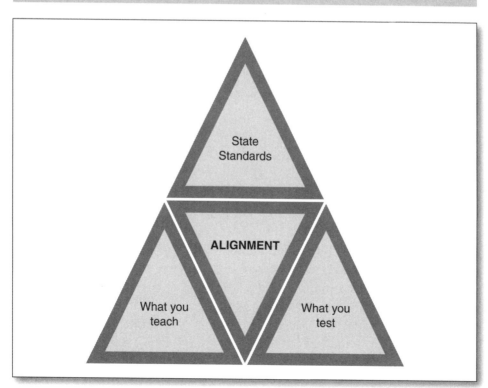

you are the expert! It would be appropriate to approach your building- or district-level reading person to begin spearheading this work. Practically speaking, it makes the most sense for this to happen at the district level so there is continuity across schools. For example, if your state standards dictate that fifth-grade students will apply reading strategies to a variety of genres and the reading program adopted by your district does not address multiple genres evenly, there is a lack of alignment.

These alignment studies can also be referred to as validity studies and can take many forms (e.g., Baker, 2004; Bhola, Impara, & Buckendahl, 2003; Rothman, 2003; Webb, 1999), but most alignment studies require at their core an item-to-standard mapping in which individual test items are evaluated with respect to one or more academic content standards.

Conducting Your Alignment Study

Step 1: Understand What You're Expected to Teach

The first thing you should do is go online to the state department website and print off a copy of your state's academic content standards for reading. Some states embed the reading standards by grade in a larger section called "English Language Arts," and some states separate them out by reading, writing, listening, speaking, and/or viewing, and then each grade-level indicator is outlined by subject. But every state's department of education website has a link to the reading standards. As an example of what you are looking for, Table 1.1 is the set of standards for English Language Arts developed by the National Council for Teachers of English (NCTE) and the International Reading Association (IRA). These were written to serve as guidelines for the state teams of educators who, in turn, each wrote their own set of grade-level expectations, state by state.

The standards documents are then broken down into grade-level expectations. Find the grade you teach, and focus on the four or five pages that describe what students should know and be able to do in reading. Especially in the primary grades, some states have a heavy emphasis on concepts in print, while others focus on vocabulary. The standards and grade-level indicators list the expectations at each grade level and are designed to help schools make curricular decisions. The reports that go to the U.S. Department of Education about student achievement in each state are based on alignment studies that are conducted using these grade-by-grade performance standards.

Know how reading is defined in your state, and don't assume that it's the same as the last place you taught. In fact, the definitions for reading, language arts, and literacy differ significantly from state to state. For example, the Iowa Core Curriculum references K–12 *literacy* standards,

Table 1.1 Standards for the English Language Arts Sponsored by NCTE and IRA

1. Students read a wide range of print and non-print texts to build an understanding of texts, of themselves, and of the cultures of the United States and the world; to acquire new information; to respond to the needs and demands of society and the workplace; and for personal fulfillment. Among these texts are fiction and nonfiction, classic and contemporary works.

2. Students read a wide range of literature from many periods in many genres to build an understanding of the many dimensions (e.g., philosophical, ethical, aesthetic) of human experience.

3. Students apply a wide range of strategies to comprehend, interpret, evaluate, and appreciate texts. They draw on their prior experience, their interactions with other readers and writers, their knowledge of word meaning and of other texts, their word identification strategies, and their understanding of textual features (e.g., sound-letter correspondence, sentence structure, context, graphics).

4. Students adjust their use of spoken, written, and visual language (e.g., conventions, style, vocabulary) to communicate effectively with a variety of audiences and for different purposes.

5. Students employ a wide range of strategies as they write and use different writing process elements appropriately to communicate with different audiences for a variety of purposes.

6. Students apply knowledge of language structure, language conventions (e.g., spelling and punctuation), media techniques, figurative language, and genre to create, critique, and discuss print and non-print texts.

7. Students conduct research on issues and interests by generating ideas and questions, and by posing problems. They gather, evaluate, and synthesize data from a variety of sources (e.g., print and non-print texts, artifacts, people) to communicate their discoveries in ways that suit their purpose and audience.

8. Students use a variety of technological and information resources (e.g., libraries, databases, computer networks, video) to gather and synthesize information and to create and communicate knowledge.

9. Students develop an understanding of and respect for diversity in language use, patterns, and dialects across cultures, ethnic groups, geographic regions, and social roles.

10. Students whose first language is not English make use of their first language to develop competency in the English language arts and to develop understanding of content across the curriculum.

11. Students participate as knowledgeable, reflective, creative, and critical members of a variety of literacy communities.

12. Students use spoken, written, and visual language to accomplish their own purposes (e.g., for learning, enjoyment, persuasion, and the exchange of information).

SOURCE: www.ncte.org/standards

and defines literacy as the ability to read, write, speak, listen, and think effectively. In contrast, Michigan has grade-level content expectations for English language arts, which defines English language arts in four strands: reading, writing, speaking, and strand four, which combines listening and viewing. In Texas, the entire domain is defined as English language arts and reading. No matter what nomenclature is used, rest assured that the high-stakes reading tests that are given in each state are aligned to the standards.

Common Core State Standards

In addition to your individual state standards for reading, there are a set of Common Core Standards that were designed to be adopted by all fifty states. The Common Core State Standards initiative was started in 2009 by the National Governors Association Center for Best Practices and the Council of Chief State School Officers to create a set of common, inter-state curricular goals for K–12 English language arts and mathematics. The standards are expected to exist alongside the state standards, not to supplant them. The Common Core State Standards (hereafter, Common Core Standards) is available online at http://www.corestandards.org

To date, forty-two states have adopted the Common Core Standards. Five states have not adopted the standards but have a timeline for reviewing and possible adoption. Three states (Alaska, Texas, and Virginia) have indicated that they do not plan on adopting the standards at all. The website: http://www.corestandards.org/in-the-states lists each state (and the District of Columbia) and their status with respect to adopting the Common Core Standards.

Really, the question is how will the Common Core Standards affect the way reading is taught across the United States? Many states already have a thoughtful, purposeful set of reading standards and grade-level expectations. If you are teaching in one of those states, you will find that the core curriculum subsumes your existing standards. In other words, what students must know and be able to do in reading according to the Common Core Standards is most likely very close to your existing state standards. Beginning in 2014, as national assessments are launched to measure the Common Core Standards so states can be compared to one another, it will be essential that teachers and administrators are able to articulate the curriculum alignment with a gap analysis.

Step 2: What Are You Teaching? Performing a Gap Analysis

Once the standards are in hand, teachers will need to look at the reading program and curriculum to perform a gap analysis. A gap analysis will show you any discrepancies between the intended curriculum, or what standards mandate students learn in classrooms, and the enacted curriculum, or what is actually being taught. To do this, consider these two questions:

1. Are all standards and/or grade-level benchmarks addressed by the curriculum?

2. Are you spending inordinate amounts of time on content that the standards and/or grade-level benchmarks do not mandate?

Teachers, along with other curriculum experts within their school, can address these questions by comparing the state standards to the curriculum being taught (See Figure 1.2). Now that you have familiarized yourself with the grade-level expectations in your state standards, you can check off the statements that represent what you already teach. When you are finished, you can see what is left.

Gaps between the **intended curriculum** (what the state department of education expects is being taught) and the **enacted curriculum** (what actually is taught) can sometimes explain low test scores.

Table 1.2 is an example of a gap analysis in which the reading standards are not all present in the test itself. One test will simply not give all of the information you want about your students. Of course students need to know how to modify predictions about forthcoming information, but as this gap analysis shows, this will not be formally assessed.

Figure 1.2 Steps to Alignment

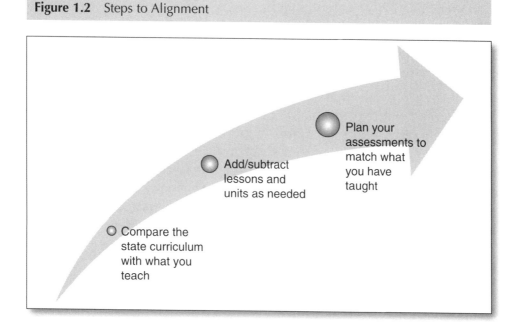

Table 1.2 Example of a Gap Analysis Where the Reading Standards Are Not All Present in the Test Itself

Reading Standard	Aligned Test Items*
Structural features of informational materials 3.1 Use titles, tables of contents, chapter headings, glossaries, and indexes to locate information in text.	Reference materials Items 1–25
Comprehension and analysis of *grade-level-appropriate* text 3.2 Connect prior knowledge with literal information found in, and inferred from, the text.	Reading comprehension: Items 5, 14, 15, 16
3.3 Demonstrate comprehension by identifying answers in the text.	Reading comprehension: Items 3, 6, 7, 10, 11, 18, 19, 20, 21, 22, 23, 24, 25, 26, 27, 30, 32
3.4 Modify predictions about forthcoming information.	
3.5 Distinguish the main idea and supporting details in expository text.	Reading comprehension: Items 8, 17, 33
3.6 Follow simple multiple-step written instructions (e.g., how to assemble a product or play a board game).	

*Examples and items listed in Table 1.2 are for illustrative purposes only.

The tricky balance is to avoid having the test drive your curriculum but still make sure you teach everything in the state standards.

Step 3: After the Gap Analysis: Modify Your Curriculum

It's very possible that your analysis will reveal gaps between the intended and enacted curriculum. But wait! Before the entire reading curriculum in your school is scrapped in exchange for a full-blown test-preparation package, check to see if some smaller adjustments can be made by adding a unit or a few lessons in the areas that are going to be tested. Sometimes adding a few lessons can go a long way toward making sure you have taught everything that is going to be on the test. For example, maybe the grade-level indicators for third grade say that students will use various strategies to figure out the meaning of vocabulary in context. Perhaps this is a standard you can't check off, because you do not have a specific set of lessons devoted to explicitly teaching vocabulary in context.

Because this will most likely also appear on the state assessment, it is imperative that the lessons you teach throughout the year have embedded within them a way to teach vocabulary in context.

One example of an activity that can help teach vocabulary in context is a bookmark-making session. Have your class create individual bookmarks for use with independent reading. The bookmark lists helpful suggestions and strategies students can use when they come to a word they don't know in the text. Cut strips of bookmark-sized paper and have the students write *STUCK?* at the top. Conduct a class brainstorming session to compile a list of strategies for good readers to use when they come to a word they do not know. Here are a few ideas to get you and your class started:

- Skip the word and read to the end of the sentence. See if the sentence still makes sense without that word. If so, keep reading.
- Go back and re-read the word and try to substitute a word that would make sense. What context clues can you use?
- Look the word up in the dictionary or ask someone. Some readers keep a list of words they don't know so they can look them up later.

Figure 1.3 shows what each different-colored construction paper strip should look like. The big one (STUCK?) goes on the bottom, and then each strip gets put on top of the other so the big words at the top are visible. When the strips are stacked in order, put a staple in the middle along the bottom.

Figure 1.3   Example of Stuck Strategies

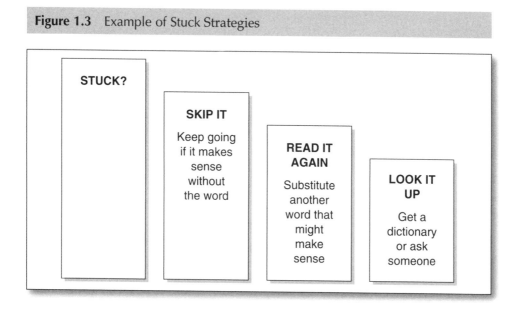

> **Definition of summative assessment:** A cumulative assessment that summarizes the accumulation of knowledge to that point. Can be used to grade student achievement in a course.

Our district adopted a new reading core program about four years ago. Since its implementation, we have struggled as a staff to ensure that it meets all the needs addressed in our state standards. After conducting our gap analysis, one area that popped up right away was that our standards called for students to apply comprehension strategies to a variety of literary genres. The reading program did a thorough job of addressing different reading strategies, but it did so almost solely with fiction selections. We immediately felt that our students were missing out by not practicing these strategies on nonfiction texts as well. As a way to address this gap, I decided to implement a nonfiction reading station for students to complete during reading groups. I conducted a reading session with each differentiated group and addressed the skills necessary to successfully read nonfiction, such as using titles, introductions, headings, captions, and other text features. After I introduced these text features during group time, I was able to have a nonfiction station. At the station, using sticky notes, students were required to label different text features and explain their purpose in a science text. This was quick and easy to assess. By looking at the sticky notes at the end of the day, I could assess each student's nonfiction reading. If students needed additional help, I could pull them back for a few minutes the next day to re-teach. At the end of the week, I gave each student a copy of a magazine article. They had to highlight and label different text features as well as explain their purpose. I felt comfortable that by doing this, along with implementing the core reading program, I was adequately addressing the state standard.

TEACHING TO THE TEST: JUST SAY NO

Let's talk about *best practice* in spite of testing.

There is a difference between teaching to the test and teaching what is going to be on the test. Popham (2005) wrote that if a teacher is "teaching to the content represented by the test" it is good teaching, but if a teacher is directing instruction specifically toward the items on the test, it is bad instruction (p. 312). If a high-stakes test is going to measure the students' abilities to find facts from a passage, or make inferences about characters, then by all means practice that in class. The state test should serve as a

summative assessment that provides evidence of how the students are growing from year to year. This can only happen if what you teach all year is in line with what is going to being tested.

Sometimes defining what exactly constitutes teaching to the test becomes muddled, or at least it does in my school. One such example happened recently as we were preparing our students for a district assessment. One of the skills tested was reading and interpreting data from a table or chart. The item on the test presented information on the levels of hurricanes in chart form. It then asked the students five multiple-choice questions based on the chart. The week before the test, a colleague placed something in my box she thought would be "useful" in helping my students practice this skill for the test.

I almost fell over when I saw a chart in the exact same format as the one presented on the test. The one difference: this chart listed the categories of tornadoes rather than hurricanes. She had also included, for my convenience, five multiple-choice questions that looked very similar to those on the test. OK, they were *exactly* the same. Question 1 on the district test asked the wind speed of a Category 2 hurricane, and Question 1 on this "review sheet" asked the wind speed of an F2 tornado. I couldn't believe it, and when I made a flip comment about teaching to the test, she seemed hurt and confused. She really didn't think this was teaching to the test!

No, I did not use this with my students, but I knew I didn't need to use it. I had addressed reading a chart and table for information earlier in the reading unit, and I knew that no matter what format or type of information was on the chart, my students could apply the concepts they had learned to read a chart on a test. I was not preparing them *just* to take the test; I truly want them to know how to read a chart, any chart.

Figure 1.4 illustrates the interactions between what is taught and what is tested. When the state content standards drive what is taught in the classrooms, then there is tight alignment between the enacted curriculum and the intended curriculum. Things get out of whack when the tests drive what is being taught. If there is already a tenuous link between the tests and the standards, then allowing the tests to drive instruction only makes it harder for the standards to have any relationship to what is being taught. In other words, as soon as you start teaching to the test, you stop teaching the essence of what you are supposed to be teaching.

Most people find it helpful to think about curriculum standards in terms of the traditional Bloom's (1956) taxonomy (see Figure 1.5). Typically, this is represented visually as a pyramid, with *Evaluation* appearing at the top and *Knowledge* at the bottom. My friend, Superintendent Narda Murphy, prefers

Figure 1.4 In your school, what is driving instruction? The state content standards or the tests?

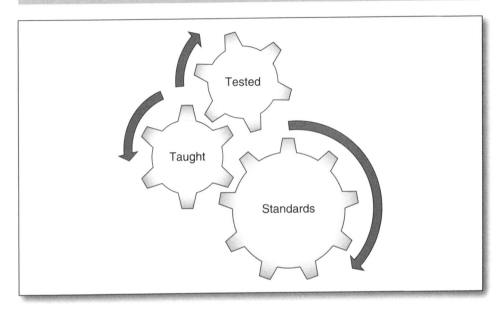

Figure 1.5 Bloom's Taxonomy, 1956

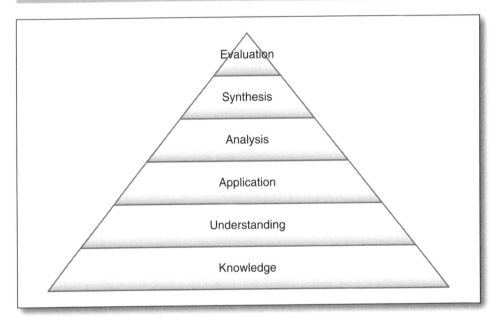

the vision of the taxonomy as a tree (see Figure 1.6), because it more accurately illustrates the idea that the very crucial roots of the tree, *Knowledge*, are required for the tree to exist at all, and without strong branches, there is nothing upon which *Evaluation* can rest.

Figure 1.6 Bloom's Taxonomy as a Tree

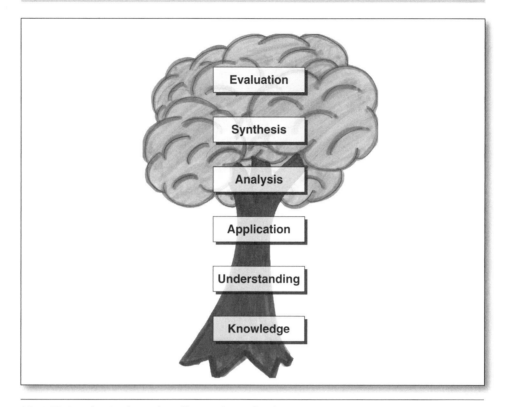

SOURCE: Tree drawing by Emily Hollingworth. Used with permission.

Our literacy team struggled with this at my school. As defined by Webb in 1999 in *Depth-of-Knowledge Levels for Four Content Areas*, it is important to align the depth of knowledge intended in the standards with that in the enacted curriculum. If a standard states that students should *evaluate* an author's use of text features and your curriculum only has students *label* such text features on a worksheet, then the depth of knowledge does not align, which means there is not alignment between standard and curriculum. To correct for this misalignment, teachers can easily adapt their current curriculum. While working on text features, it is important to discuss the relevance and uses of the features in different types of texts and where each feature is best placed so readers can easily access and understand the information provided in the text. A teacher can present examples of good and bad uses of text features, discussing with the students why each example is either good or bad. By adding this small activity (see Table 1.3) you have now aligned your teaching with the intended depth of knowledge in the state standards.

Table 1.3 Webb's Depth of Knowledge

Level 1 Recall	Recall of a fact, information, or procedure
Level 2 Skill/concept	Use information or conceptual knowledge, two or more steps
Level 3 Strategic thinking	Requires reasoning, developing plan or a sequence of steps, some complexity, more than one possible answer
Level 4 Extended thinking	Requires an investigation, time to think and process multiple conditions of the problem

SOURCE: Based on Webb (2002).

KEY POINTS TO REMEMBER

Alignment studies of content standards and test items are the key to demonstrating program validity to states. Be sure that what you are teaching matches up with the expectations spelled out in the state standards documents. Educate yourself on the extent to which your classroom curriculum aligns with the state test by conducting a gap analysis. Use this information to make decisions about ways you can adjust your curriculum so that the tests match up with what you are teaching. When teachers fully understand and teach to the state standards, then there is no danger of teaching to the test. Clearly, you should teach what is going to be *on* the test, but that's just not the same as a test-preparation curriculum, is it? Remember that there are many worthwhile literacy goals in those standards that are not going to be on the test (think: instilling a lifelong love of reading). That does *not* mean you should ignore them!

END-OF-CHAPTER QUIZ
(ANSWERS ARE IN THE BACK OF THE BOOK)

In May, when Mrs. Brown is looking over her class's scores on the state high-stakes grammar test, she notices that all of her third graders but one missed an item about capitalizing the name of a city. Although the items on the test are not released to the public, she got a copy of the test from her school counselor, who had one squirreled away in her desk. She knows that this form of the test won't be given again next year, but the items themselves might show up again on future versions of the test.

The item read as follows

A. *Becky and her family are going*

B. *to visit her grandparents*

C. *in louisville, Kentucky*

D. *this summer.*

E. *No mistakes*

An item analysis revealed that fifteen of her students chose B as the answer, one chose C, and ten chose E.

What, ethically, should Mrs. Brown do with this knowledge? Here are some suggestions from a group of teachers for you to ponder:

1. Well, clearly she can't just give next year's kids that same item to practice. She could, however, make up a worksheet of lots of other items that are clones of this one. Like instead of *Becky* it's *Jose*—and instead of visiting her grandparents, it could be her aunt—and the city and state could be different. Would that be ok?

2. She could look over all of her old lesson plans and see whether or not she even taught the capitalization of cities last year. If she did, then the lessons definitely didn't work. She should figure out how to expand her old lessons, maybe with some map work in geography class, to familiarize students with important cities in each state.

3. Who cares? It's just one item. Were there other city-and-state capitalization items on the same test that the kids got *right*?

4. She should check out the state standards and make sure that capitalizing cities is a grade-level expectation in her state. Chances are, there are a whole series of language arts standards about capitalization, and she might have missed more than just cities and states when she figured out what to teach last year. This information could be used to rewrite her lessons for the coming year.

5. She should look to see if the other third-grade teachers had the same problem in their classes. Maybe it's a problem with the third-grade language arts curriculum. Maybe it was just the implementation of it in Mrs. Brown's room.

2 Using Formative Assessments

Chapter Highlights

- The difference between formative and summative assessments
- Using formative assessment to check learning as you go
- Using formative assessment to differentiate instruction

G ood teaching requires frequent feedback from students in the form of assessments to check not only their learning progress, but also to monitor the efficacy of the pedagogical processes selected by the teacher (Heritage, 2007). One of the ways teachers are monitoring learning is to give students formative assessments, tests, and exercises that provide teachers with data that can be used to encourage students to be self-reflective about their learning progress (Black, Harrison, Lee, Marshall, & Wiliam, 2003).

Formative assessments are generally thought of as

a. metacognitive tools designed to support instruction, and

b. tools that can facilitate the creation of a learning profile for students to track their progress over time.

The purpose of these assessments is to provide fast, daily feedback on student academic performance across the curriculum. There has been research in the field of educational measurement in the past few years on the use of formative assessments to raise standards of achievement and to achieve higher quality learning (Black, Harrison, Lee, Marshall, & Wiliam, 2004; Black & Wiliam, 1998a). Stiggins (2002) has called for the use of classroom assessments both in the service of student learning and as a tool for school improvement. Specifically, he argues that teachers can glean valuable information about student learning when the quality of teacher-developed classroom assessments is sound. Popham (2008) goes so far as to call this new way to think about assessment as *transformative assessment*. In this model, educators identify **learning progressions** (the sequence set of subskills a student will learn in a given unit of study) and invent ways to ascertain the extent to which students have mastered them (**formative assessments**). This stands in contrast to more traditional ways of assessing student knowledge at the end of a unit of study (**summative assessments**), and is different from the once a year high-stakes state tests that are used for state accountability reporting purposes. Rather, *assessment for learning*, as conceived by Black et al. (2003), is an approach to teaching that includes embedded activities that provide the teachers with ongoing feedback on student learning.

In this chapter, the research base for formative assessments is outlined and an explanation of different approaches to analyzing test scores for various purposes, such as **differentiated instruction**, is given.

WHAT DOES *FORMATIVE* MEAN?

Formative assessments are tests that encourage students to be self-reflective. Teachers use the data from formative assessments to create a learning profile for students to track their progress over time. The Council of Chief State School Officers (CCSSO) defines formative assessment on their website (http://tinyurl.com/3mgazca) this way: "Formative assessment is a process used by teachers and students during instruction that provides feedback to adjust ongoing teaching and learning to improve students' achievement of intended instructional outcomes."

There is ample research evidence for the power of formative assessment practices, over time, to raise standards of achievement and to lead to higher quality learning (see for example a meta-analysis of about 250 studies conducted by Black & Wiliam, 1998a). The most common result of this research is the finding that successful teachers find ways to use assessment evidence to adapt their teaching to meet student learning needs.

In one example of a formative assessment, teachers hold individual conferences with students to discuss performance on classroom assessments. In this way, student strengths and weaknesses can be identified and strategies for improvement can be developed. These conferences are also an ideal opportunity for goal setting, which we will discuss further in Chapter 4.

At my elementary school, we use three writing prompts for our district standard-based assessments. The fall prompt, generally given in classes the first week or two of school, is used as baseline data, and the spring and winter prompts are used to determine proficiency. After each prompt, I spend a language class period going over the prompts and the student scores as a whole class. I have a form where students mark their scores in each trait and overall performance. On the form, they set goals for the next prompt and outline which specific writing traits they will focus on during writing workshops for the next few months. I use the same form each time so students can track their growth and I can focus instruction and class time based on needs. I also use the forms to drive our discussions during individual student writing conferences. With curriculum-based, formative assessments, academic goals for the students are made clear before, during, and after a unit of instruction, allowing teachers to target specific lessons to just the students who need them. The results of these formative assessments can also be reported to parents to help them see a trajectory of student learning throughout the year.

I do this in my differentiated reading groups. The groups are flexible and constantly change throughout the year based on different data from formative assessments. At any one point, I may have a group working on r-controlled vowels, word attack strategies in multisyllabic words, or evaluating a text. These groups are formed based on my observation in the classroom, student performance on weekly skills tests, and classroom work. Students in each group are very aware of the targeted skill for that week. It is explicitly stated at the beginning of each group's lesson, and students are told why this skill is important to becoming better readers. Students are also made aware why they are in a particular group, for example, if I noticed them miscuing words in a running record, or if they struggled with evaluating on the last class assignment. At the end of the week before moving on to the next targeted skill, I have to know whether my students have acquired this targeted skill. To do this, I use formative assessments. By having the students in my r-controlled vowel group decode nonsense words containing r-controlled vowels, I can determine if the skill has been mastered. If the student has understood, he or she will move on to the next gap or need. If not, the student will spend more time focusing on that skill.

Despite the available research base supporting the power of formative assessment processes to improve teaching and learning, these practices are not necessarily being implemented in classrooms (Black & Wiliam, 1998b; Harlen & James, 1997). The trouble, according to educators like Rick Stiggins, is that new teachers are graduating from preparation programs that have left them underprepared to develop sound classroom assessments that can be used for student learning (Stiggins, 1999), and many veteran teachers are not exactly sure what it means to use assessment for student learning.

There is an art to creating a classroom culture where students freely discuss their learning processes in terms of learning goals. Teachers who keep running records know that the data collection and monitoring systems are key to staying organized.

The success criteria come from the learning goals, and the formative assessment strategies are what inform the teaching. The zone of proximal development (Vygotsky, 1978) is the *sweet spot* where a student is on this continuum, or learning progression. In teacher training, we teach preservice teachers that the zone of proximal development is "the distance between a child's actual developmental level as determined through independent problem solving and potential development as determined through problem solving under adult guidance or a collaboration with more capable peers" (Vygotsky, 1978, p. 86).

Figure 2.1 illustrates a way to conceptualize learning progressions in general.

For a specific example, let's pretend that a third-grade teacher, Ms. Engel, wants to teach students how to find the main idea from an expository text (Figure 2.2).

This is an important standard to teach at any grade. Ms. Engel's first step is to figure out what kinds of knowledge a student needs in order to find the main idea. Well, depending on whether the text is from a newspaper article, a passage from a history book, a piece of expository text from an encyclopedia, or an excerpt from an opinion essay, the main idea might present itself to the reader in different places physically in the text. Ms. Engel's students will need to have sufficient background knowledge on different text genres. They will have to master the ability to dissect passages from various genres and to know where the main idea is usually found. From there, the students will have to be able to retell the main idea using their own words.

What makes assessment for learning different is that the classroom assessments given are used to help both the teacher and the students see the trajectory of intended learning. For this reason, it is critical that the teacher find ways to take apart the standards for learning and find ways to both teach and assess those standards.

Learning progressions provide teachers with the knowledge and key skills in a carefully constructed pathway.

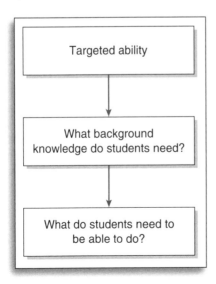

Figure 2.1 Learning Progression Model

For example, what are the skills needed to understand text structures? These are organized into a scheme. The plural of schema is schemata. Piaget (1972) called schemata the building blocks of thinking. Once you have an integrated curriculum, you can design the lessons based on the learning progression. That progression then is a series of steps that increase in complexity over time. The level of detail (granularity) and time span for the learning progression may be different depending on your needs. If you are looking at 180 days in Grade 3, that's going to be a different learning progression than one built for K–6.

There is no need to reinvent the wheel when looking for guidance in outlining your own learning progression for reading. Here is a well-known model to get you started.

Figure 2.2 Learning Progression Example in Reading: Finding the *Main Idea*

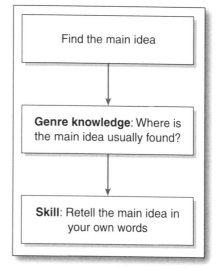

Find the main idea

↓

Genre knowledge: Where is the main idea usually found?

↓

Skill: Retell the main idea in your own words

Chall's Stages of Reading Development

Jeanne Chall's (1983) model of the stages of reading acquisition readily lends itself to be used as a scaffold for a progression of learning development. In Chall's model, each stage builds on skills mastered in earlier stages; lack of mastery at any level can halt the progress beyond that level.

- **Stage 0. Pre-reading**: The learner gains familiarity with the language and its sounds. A person in this stage becomes aware of sound similarities between words, learns to predict the next part in a familiar story, and may start to recognize a few familiar written words. Chall's Stage 0 is considered comparable to what is often called *reading readiness*. Typically developing readers achieve this stage about the age of five or six.
- **Stage 1. Initial reading stage, or decoding stage**: The reader becomes aware of the relationship between sounds and letters and begins applying the knowledge to text. In this stage, the reader has achieved an understanding of the concept of the alphabetic code and is learning sound-symbol correspondences. Typically developing readers usually reach this stage by the age of six or seven.

- **Stage 2. Confirmation**: This stage involves confirming the knowledge acquired in the previous two stages and gaining fluency in those skills. Decoding skills continue to improve, and they begin to develop speed in addition to accuracy in word recognition. At this point, the reader should be able to give attention both to meaning and to the print, using them interactively to build their skills and fluency. This stage is critical for the beginning reader. If the developing reader stops making progress during this stage, the individual remains, in Chall's words, "glued to the print." Typically developing readers usually reach this stage around the age of seven or eight.
- **Stage 3. Reading to learn**: At this stage, the motivation for reading changes. The reader has enough reading skill to begin to read text in order to gain information. Readers' vocabulary development accelerates at this point resulting from increased exposure to the written word. Typically developing children usually achieve this stage around the age of nine or ten.
- **Stage 4. Multiple viewpoints**: Readers at this stage begin to be able to analyze what they read, understand different points of view, and react critically to what they read. Typical readers are developing this ability to see text from multiple viewpoints during the high school years, around ages fourteen to nineteen.
- **Stage 5. Construction and judgment**: At this stage, readers have learned to read selectively and form their own opinions about what they read. They construct their knowledge from that of others, in this case, from what they read. This highest level of reading development is not usually reached until college age or later, and may in fact be achieved only by those who have an intellectual inclination.

Once you have established a model of reading acquisition that works for you, it is time to build a learning progression, which is the foundation of using assessment for learning.

Steps for Building Learning Progressions

1. Locate the essential concept in reading that appears across multiple grades in the state curriculum. For example:
   - Use multiple decoding strategies.
   - Read independently for pleasure.
   - Read for learning across content areas.
   - Use multiple strategies to develop and expand reading vocabulary.

2. Think about what learning looks like at each level. What behaviors do you expect to observe in students at each stage of learning?

3. Do the concepts become increasingly complex across the progression? What are the major building blocks that are addressed? Are the building blocks linked in ways that help build skills?

4. Design success criteria based on the learning goals. What can a student who has mastered a skill know and be able to do at each stage?

5. What kind of instructional strategy are you as the teacher going to provide to make sure the student really understands the material? What is the question or questions you are going to pose to the student to check understanding? The questions we pose to students are the formative assessment.

6. Have additional teaching strategies ready to re-teach if the student doesn't understand or is having trouble demonstrating the success criteria. What differentiated tasks do you have in your toolbox to help students progress through the building blocks?

Another important point to note is that the kinds of questions that are asked on formative assessments should require students to think about their own reading and learning processes, and not just recall the text. As Allington (2001) points out, adults do not quiz one another about facts from magazine articles they just read, they discuss them. Classroom literacy assessments should model this kind of real-world pattern of making connections to texts and self via conversations, rather than just recalling facts from texts (we'll talk more about real-world strategies in Chapter 3).

But contrary to the research around teacher-based formative assessment models, there is a marketing movement among publishing companies looking to capitalize on this trend. These companies are creating tests for teachers, which they are selling as *formative assessments*, to somehow replace the assessments you already have built into your teaching (including observations of kids in small groups and individually).

Don't waste your money. *Any* test can be used as a formative assessment. A test, in and of itself, is not either formative or summative. What makes a test formative is how the test results are used. Let me explain.

Say we give a spelling test to a classroom of sixth graders. It has twenty words on it. It's easy to grade it. Either the child spelled it right or he or she didn't. For you vocabulary junkies in the audience, you may be interested to know that we call that a *dichotomous* item. (True–False is a dichotomous-type item.) It's either right or it's not. If we were to use this spelling test as a formative assessment, the teacher would look at patterns of letters used by the students to see what kinds of mistakes are being made.

The information you take from this assessment could lead to the formation of reading groups. For example, say the words on the spelling test have short vowel sounds. Some of the vowel sounds are spelled with a single vowel (hen, sad, lick, pot), and others are spelled with vowel teams (bread, said, lead). As you grade the tests, you notice that a small group of your students missed only the words that used vowel teams to spell the short vowel sounds. Obviously, there is a pattern of mistakes. This group of students should be placed into a small reading group and the focus of instruction for the next week or so, or until mastery, should be short vowel sounds with vowel teams.

Without a doubt, this would help improve student learning. But there are many other choices for how to use the data from this spelling test (see Figure 2.3).

HOW ARE THE SCORES OF TEST TAKERS ANALYZED?

After the test has been given, it is time to decide how to use the information you will get from the test. Tests can be interpreted in two ways.

Criterion referenced: The teacher decides in advance what percentage of words need to be spelled correctly in order to decide if the student passed.

Norm referenced: The teacher orders the children by rank according to how many words they spelled right. The teacher then decides where to draw a line to separate the kids who pass and the kids who don't.

Figure 2.3 How Are the Scores of Test Takers Analyzed?

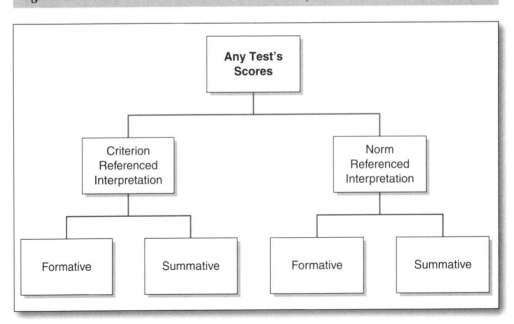

Once the teacher has decided how to analyze the scores, there is another big question to address. How will the test results be used?

Formative: Think of this as a way to check how the students are doing. If a teacher just taught something and wants to see how many of the kids have learned it, the results can be used to help the teacher identify students who need additional instructional support. If the spelling test, for example, is at the beginning of a unit to teach students about homonyms, then the test results could be used to figure out who understands what and who still doesn't get it.

You are going to find that there are lots of really smart marketing executives out there who will put the word *formative* in front of the name of a test they are selling because they think it will be a more popular product. You don't necessarily need a marketed *"formative assessment."* As we've already discussed, any test can be used as a formative assessment. If you are using test evidence to guide instruction, then you are already using a formative assessment.

Summative: When teachers use test results to decide whether kids understand something at the end of the lesson, then the test becomes a summative assessment. So if the words selected for the spelling test were a culmination of a unit of study about the rule where we drop the *e* and add *ing*, then the teacher could use the results of this spelling test to *sum up* how each student did at the end of the unit.

Once you have assessment data about where your students are along the learning progression, it is critical that you have a variety of teaching strategies in place so you can be sure to meet the needs of each individual student. This is called **differentiated instruction**.

DIFFERENTIATED INSTRUCTION

Every student develops reading fluency at a different pace. Differentiated instruction applies an approach to teaching and learning so that students have multiple options for learning. In a reading classroom, teachers can accomplish this by creating numerous opportunities for students to work in groups with flexible membership based on interest and ability. In this way, the reading process can be scaffolded, or provide a tiered platform to be used, not only by the teacher but also by other students in the groups. The use of assessments for determining differentiated instructional needs will keep group membership fluid. Many teachers get caught in the trap of *"tracking"* students who never truly have a chance to move out of their group.

The critical component of differentiated instruction is assessment. How do you know what your students know and are able to do if you do not have a way to measure it? Tomlinson and Cunningham-Eidson (2003) write that the three characteristics students need are readiness to learn, interest or motivation, and the student's learning profile, or mode of learning. The teacher differentiates, or modifies, teaching to fit each student's individual needs. The formative assessment tools used by teachers to make the decisions about differentiation might be teacher-made tests, performance activities, or some other kind of assessment that gives a snapshot of what the student knows and is able to do.

TESTS AS A SNAPSHOT: THE JACUZZI METAPHOR

Either way, it's probably worth saying something here about my Jacuzzi. Trust me. It's relevant.

There are lots of things I want to know about the water in my Jacuzzi before I get into it (see Figure 2.4). Is the water clean? Do I need to add any chemicals? How hot is the water? Is there anything broken? Is the water a funky color? Is that mold growing on the bottom?! Any one test is only going to tell me a little bit about all of the things I want to know. Before I get in, I'm going to need to test the pH, the chlorine level, and I'm really going to want to look at the filter.

A twenty-word spelling test is the equivalent of sticking your finger in the hot tub and deciding whether or not it's good enough to go in.

It doesn't matter whether you report the results as criterion or normed or if you use the results for formative or summative purposes. It doesn't matter if it's a teacher-made test or a statewide assessment. In the end, any one test can only give you a *snapshot* of what your students can do. You need to balance the information you get from that twenty-word test (or your finger in the Jacuzzi) with all of the other information you already have. If I already tested the chlorine yesterday—and the pool guy already came out this month to check the filters, and it doesn't look slimy in there—then I'm OK with just sticking my finger in and jumping in if it feels warm. But I would not tell you that one of my students is proficient at spelling if all I had to go on was a "finger-dip" twenty-word spelling test.

The most pervasive example of a finger-dip test is the DIBELS.

DIBELS

One of the more popular reading tests being given in elementary schools for diagnostic purposes is the Dynamic Indicators of Basic Early Literacy Skills (DIBELS). DIBELS is a quick (the whole battery can be administered in less

Figure 2.4 My Jacuzzi Tests

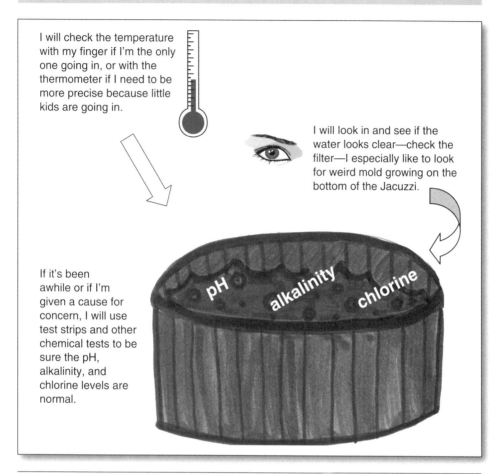

I will check the temperature with my finger if I'm the only one going in, or with the thermometer if I need to be more precise because little kids are going in.

I will look in and see if the water looks clear—check the filter—I especially like to look for weird mold growing on the bottom of the Jacuzzi.

If it's been awhile or if I'm given a cause for concern, I will use test strips and other chemical tests to be sure the pH, alkalinity, and chlorine levels are normal.

pH   alkalinity   chlorine

SOURCE: Jacuzzi drawing by Emily Hollingworth. Used with permission.

than nine minutes), relatively inexpensive test of a child's ability to read out loud. Anyone with an hour of training can administer the test; you don't even need expertise in reading. After a student reads the test aloud to the test administrator, scores describing the mechanical aspects of reading are issued. This might include initial sounds, phoneme segmentation fluency, nonsense word fluency, letter-naming fluency, and oral-reading fluency. Scores are based on the speed with which the text is read aloud. The school administrators who are using the DIBELS in their districts really like the fact that (a) it does not take a lot of class time to administer and (b) it is very easy to use.

Unfortunately, DIBELS is a finger-dip test. It is not a test that can provide teachers with information about where students are along the reading acquisition continuum. DIBELS does not provide students with the opportunity to demonstrate reading comprehension skills or the ability to make personal connections to text. In addition, students who are not naturally oral readers are at a disadvantage because of the format of the test.

The DIBELS makes me think of the movie, *Anchorman*, where Will Farrell's character, Ron Burgundy, reads the news fluidly from a tele-prompter but never has any idea what he's saying. This makes him ripe for a very funny prank where the words are changed and he unthinkingly reads the new words. This prank demonstrates his poor literacy skills, despite his oral fluency.

The biggest problem with DIBELS isn't the test itself but rather that school districts are using the results of these tests, and these tests alone, to make important decisions about whether or not a student is having diffi-culty reading. Many experts in reading and language acquisition theory have expressed their dissatisfaction with the way the DIBELS has been used as a tool for measuring reading (Afflerbach, 2007; Goodman, 2006). Several researchers have conducted research studies into the lack of valid-ity evidence for using DIBELS scores as a measure for evaluating a literacy instructional program (Kamii & Manning, 2005).

What to Do If the DIBELS Is Part of Your Assessment System

So let's pretend you are in a school district that uses the scores on the DIBELS to decide who qualifies for special education. What steps can you take to ensure more accurate and reliable assessments? First and foremost, I recommend that you arm yourself with Goodman's book, *The Truth About DIBELS: What It Is, What It Does* (Goodman, 2006). In it, he and his coau-thors argue that the authors of the test "believe that competent reading is the ability to read words rapidly and accurately and that comprehension is the result of such rapid, accurate reading." The authors also believe that "what happens in one minute of reading happens in all of reading" (p. 10). In addition to providing the reader with an excellent line of logic to argue with school administrators about what DIBELS does and does not do, the book also comes with a PowerPoint presentation on a CD, to use as a con-versation guide with staff.

After reading that book, you may be inspired to give anyone who will listen your opinion of the DIBELS as a progress monitor for anything besides oral reading. In the past two or three years, I have spoken at con-ferences with many teachers and school principals who don't understand how a test like this has become so widely misused as a test of reading comprehension. Unfortunately, the reason why DIBELS is so popular is mainly due to its low cost and ease of use. Talk to the decision makers in your school district about ways to monitor progress that don't cost money, don't compromise your integrity as a literacy instructor, and are in align-ment with ways we define reading comprehension.

This has proven to be a very frustrating discussion for me, because the test scores seem to carry more weight than my expert teacher opinion. I have tried, and continue to try, to talk with the literacy coordinator at my school regarding our use of DIBELS. I am constantly assured that we are not using DIBELS alone to make decisions about the needs of our students. However, every year I feel I have to *"go to bat"* for some of my students who happen to be slower readers, the ones who scored "Strategic or Intensive" on DIBELS but are actually phenomenal readers and score "Proficient" or "Advanced" on our district or state assessments. These students are always recommended for pull-out programs such as Read Naturally to improve fluency or a phonics program to fill any necessary holes. To me, if we weren't solely using DIBELS data then we would have the benefit of data from other assessments to inform our decisions.

The last thing I'll say about the DIBELS is this: it received a scathing review in the *The Sixteenth Mental Measurement Yearbook* (MMY) (see Good et al., 2002–2003). The MMY is a publication filled with reviews of tests in print from psychometricians and content experts who know what good testing is and what it is not. I highly recommend to every school district that you pay for a subscription to the online version (http://www.unl.edu/buros/), which gives you access to all of the test reviews. Any off-the-shelf test that your district is thinking of purchasing will appear in this book. If you are looking at a test that has *not* been peer reviewed in MMY, then you should be aware that it has not been subjected to any kind of rigorous scrutiny of its validity or reliability, and you would be advised to carefully consider using it in your own classroom. Usually, there are two reviews for each test in print, and the reviewers go through everything from the way the test looks to the interpretation manuals. The more information about the technical quality of an instrument that you can get your hands on, the better your chances of making informed decisions about which tests to purchase.

DIBELS is, after all, just a finger-dip test. When a student is flagged by his or her score on the DIBELS, I then conduct a more in-depth investigation to find out why that student is reading slower than the grade-level benchmark set by the DIBELS people. For the lowest-scoring students, I usually give a phonics assessment to determine if there are any holes. If so, I'll start the year working on phonics in small groups. If students are quick to pick up the phonics concepts, then we can move along. If a phonics test comes back *"clean,"* I move on to the next theory as to why their reading is not hitting the mark. My next step would be a little instruction in fluency, which could become the next focus of small-group instruction. We would work on chunking, grouping portions of text into short, meaningful phrases, using punctuation to pause and determine meaning, and punctuation to determine expression. Sometimes, though, fluency isn't the problem either, and at that point, then your teaching strategies will come from your knowledge base about how students become fluent oral readers.

As a professional development activity with your colleagues, brainstorm all the ways you both formally and informally measure the reading skills of your students. Then, classify each assessment using the Jacuzzi metaphor as a guide. The goal is for you to have a conversation about the need for **multiple measures** to get the most accurate picture of student ability. Relying on one snapshot from one moment in time to make important instructional decisions is simply not best practice.

TEST QUALITY AND DISTRICT ASSESSMENTS

Over the past eight years, most of the reading teachers I have met and observed in the classroom have developed a thoughtful and purposeful set of their own classroom tests, from a combination of workbooks, online resources, textbooks, and lessons borrowed from colleagues. Those who have been given the gift of time to work in professional groups with other teachers to build these assessments into a formalized system are the ones who are leading the way in teacher-developed formative assessments. These teachers can tell you what knowledge their students are developing in a given unit of study and what kind of thinking they want their students to be able to do; they can identify an observable performance or skill each student will be able to exhibit once he or she is proficient. In other words, they can take the learning progression model (Figure 2.1) and tell you exactly what they are going to be teaching.

In larger school districts, this ownership is sometimes taken away from the teachers and placed instead in the hands of a district reading coordinator. Sometimes, this can be a fantastic opportunity for reading teachers to have coordinated instructional leadership. But it is critical that reading coordinators have a background in assessment.

Let me tell you the story of my friend, Mrs. B., who teaches elementary school. She called me last week to tell me about the district literacy coordinator who wanted to increase the interrater reliability on the district writing assessments (which, by the way, are being called "formative"). **Reliability** is the consistency of test scores on different items that cover the same skills or the consistency of an instrument by raters or observers. **Interrater reliability** is the extent to which two different people obtain the same result when using the same instrument to measure a student's achievement (*inter* meaning "between" and *rater* meaning "someone who rates"). Interrater reliability indices are expressed as a decimal from 0 to 1, with scores closest to 1 considered to be high.

The teachers in Mrs. B's school went through a training session on how to score the writing responses. They then read the students' answers to the district-built assessment and scored them. Each writing test was read independently by two teachers. If the scores from the two reading tests did not match, then a third rater was asked to read it so a final score could be obtained. The interrater reliability coefficient that is calculated from these activities is the percentage of time the two raters got the same score. So if sixty of one hundred writing tests received the same score from the two teachers who read them, then the interrater reliability is .60. In general, the value of the interrater reliability coefficient is to give the test coordinator an idea of how successful the rater training session was. If there is a wide disagreement among the teachers about what a proficient response to the writing assessment should be, then it is time for another robust conversation with the teachers about what good writing looks like.

Here's how Mrs. B's coordinator handled it.

The district coordinator held a special meeting to tell Mrs. B's school that their interrater reliability was not as high as that of other schools in the district. The district coordinator planned to change the individual teacher ratings so that they matched more often. In the mind of the district coordinator, the interrater reliability index was somehow an important score, but the absurdity of her solution was lost on her.

So what happened when the coordinator made this announcement to the staff? Apparently, my snarky friend, Mrs. B, told the coordinator to go ahead and score them all herself, since then the interrater reliability would be 1.00.

END-OF-CHAPTER QUIZ

Your elementary school principal, Mr. Clinton, has decided to purchase a very expensive formative assessment kit, which includes graphic organizers to photocopy and scripts for you to follow during direct literacy instruction. The materials include a happy face and a frowny face for kids to keep on their desk. When they feel confused about a lesson, kids will show the sad face. When they understand it, they show the happy face. The materials also include a chart for class observations to describe how each student is doing.

At your faculty meeting, Mr. Clinton announces that every teacher will be expected to use these materials, and at the end of each week, the observation charts will be collected by him for review to ensure that the program is being followed. He says that the purpose of this program is to take stock of where students are and to help the teachers monitor student progress.

What do you do?

1. Teacher scripts?! No way! I am going to lead a full-scale revolt right here and now.

2. Wait until you have a chance to read the materials and look at some reviews of the program online. Maybe there will be something good you can use.

3. Ask Mr. Clinton what are the criterion upon which the success of this program will be measured. How will the administration be measuring the efficacy of this, admittedly, very expensive formative assessment program, and will the teachers have the opportunity to weigh in on whether or not they find the system useful in their daily practice?

4. Ask if the sixth-grade teachers have permission not to use the smiley and frowny faces, since the big kids are going to mock this openly.

5. Make sure the program allows you to continue teaching the way you have been, with group work such as literature circles, and with student-selected, high-interest texts that are grounded in real-world contexts.

6. Close your door and do whatever you were going to do anyway.

3 Struggling Readers

Chapter Highlights

- Struggling readers on individualized education programs (IEPs)
- Accommodations and modifications on reading assessments
- Using assistive technology with reading
- English language learners (ELLs)

Critics of No Child Left Behind (NCLB) write about the unintended consequences of the accountability legislation: narrowing of the curriculum, the privileging of test scores as the most important piece of evidence that students are learning, and so on. One of the *intended* consequences of NCLB is to put teacher focus on populations of students who often are underserved in American public schools. The goal of this chapter is to arm reading teachers with the knowledge needed to take advantage of the incredible opportunities that exist for students with special needs.

What do struggling readers have in common? They tend to have trouble with vocabulary, particularly in the content area. Also, they often struggle with applying background knowledge to text. For example, struggling readers find it very difficult to predict what might happen next in the story.

Here's a story:

Once upon a time there was a little boy named Luke. Luke had an IEP that gave him permission to have a teacher read classroom materials to him. One day, Luke's classroom teacher got in an argument with the special education teacher about whether or not Luke could have the special education teacher read a language arts test to him.

The answer is that it depends on what the test is for; if it's a reading test, then having it read to him becomes a modification. If it is a listening test, then the test being read to him is an accommodation.

ACCOMMODATIONS VERSUS MODIFICATIONS

So a student like Luke could definitely benefit from having a science test read out loud to him, because then his reading issues won't interfere with an assessment of his science content knowledge. **Accommodations** provide support for the student to meet the same curricular expectations as the regular education students. Accommodations are changes that don't necessarily alter the expectations for a class activity or for a test. Instead, an accommodation provides a different way for students to take in information or to communicate what they have learned back to the teacher. The purpose of an accommodation is to ensure that every student has equal access to the curriculum. This might mean extra time to take a test or an opportunity to take a test in the student's home language. Some other common accommodations include the use of scribes, and tests in Braille. The main goal of an accommodation is to help the student become independent. As a teacher, you are legally bound to implement any accommodations in a student's individualized education program (IEP). It is important that the accommodations are used regularly so that students are familiar with them and comfortable using them when testing time rolls around. It is also perfectly acceptable to allow for accommodations not called for on an IEP in your own classroom. For example, I have students that I make accommodations for, especially in science and social studies. Often, the reading level of the material we use keeps the student from accessing the material, so I will read it to them or have them listen to an audio version. While this is great in the classroom, do be careful. Unfortunately, we can't pick and choose accommodations for our students on state tests. Only allowable accommodations are permitted, and they must be included in the student's IEP.

Modifications are used to change the curricular expectations for the student. So if Luke has a reading test read to him, then what is actually being tested is Luke's ability to *listen*, not his ability to make meaning from what he reads himself. Modifications mean that the curriculum and/or the instruction is different. For example, a third grader with a reading disability may be given a modified list of spelling words to learn each week. This could be a list of words that is shorter than the rest of the class or simply easier words. Students who take *alternative assessments* instead of the NCLB state test are being given a modification. A modification doesn't give a true feel for a student's abilities; it's a different test. The results of this different test cannot be directly compared to the results of the non-modified tests that students who are in regular education take. There really isn't much most classroom teachers can do to deal with this issue. These accommodations and modifications are on the IEP when the student comes to you and, legally, that's what you do. Oftentimes, my students' annual IEPs aren't until spring, so I don't have much input into how a student's lessons will be modified in my class. All I can do is to implement these accommodations and/or modifications in my classroom in order that by the time state testing rolls around, my student is comfortable with the accommodations and/or modifications and knows what to expect.

MODIFICATIONS AND HIGH-STAKES TESTS: ALTERNATIVE ASSESSMENTS

The rules for NCLB are influenced by the requirements of the Individuals with Disabilities Education Act (IDEA, 1997). As a result, states can administer an alternative assessment to students with significant cognitive disabilities, up to 1 percent of the student population. These are assessments with different, less complex standards than those that are administered to non–learning-disabled (LD) students.

The federal policies that guide alternative assessment use can be found online at http://www.ed.gov/policy/speced/guid/modachieve-summary.html. Basically, an alternate assessment is based on modified academic achievement standards. The student must have a disability under Section 602(3) of IDEA, and may be in any of the disability categories listed in the IDEA. A student's IEP determines how the student will participate in the high-stakes state assessments (for example whether a student will have accommodations or modifications). Each state has to establish guidelines for which students qualify to take alternative assessments. Here are the official rules from the ed.gov website (http://www2.ed.gov/policy/speced/guid/modachieve-summary.html):

1. There must be objective evidence demonstrating that the student's disability has precluded the student from achieving grade-level proficiency. Such evidence may include the student's performance on State assessments or other assessments that can validly document academic achievement.

2. The student's progress to date in response to appropriate instruction, including special education and related services designed to address the student's individual needs, is such that, even if significant

growth occurs, the IEP Team is reasonably certain that the student will not achieve grade-level proficiency within the year covered by the student's IEP. The IEP Team must use multiple valid measures of the student's progress over time in making this determination.

3. The student's IEP must include goals that are based on grade-level academic content standards. It is a State's responsibility to establish and monitor implementation of clear and appropriate guidelines for IEP Teams to use when deciding if an alternate assessment based on modified academic achievement standards is appropriate for an individual student. These guidelines should provide parameters and direction to ensure that students are not assessed based on modified academic achievement standards merely because of their disability category or their racial or economic background or the lack of appropriate instruction.

A modified test might be based on a different set of academic content standards, or it might just be the same test but out-of-level—that is, a fifth grader might take the third-grade reading test. Find out how these rules have been interpreted and put into practice in your state and in your district. Make sure that you are taking advantage of the opportunities available to your special needs kids.

ACCOMMODATIONS AND HIGH-STAKES TESTS

One of the more exciting trends in special education since the 2004 IDEA is the developing technology that has led to new accommodation requests.

When state test developers create their instructions and guidelines for use and interpretation of scores, the IDEA requires that they provide a list of accommodations that won't interfere with test validity. This allows users to be sure that the test is measuring what it is supposed to measure. There are so many cool new gadgets being invented, it's hard not to want to find ways to use them to engage resistant learners.

For example, I visited a school district in rural Iowa that had purchased a few dozen iPods with video screens to use with elementary students who had IEPs that required test materials are read aloud to them. As a matter of convenience, the computer teacher hit on the idea to record the tests electronically, save it as an MP3 music file, and then allow the students to play the tests back on an iPod. The school got a grant from Apple to use iPods in educational settings, and they were heralded around the country as a school that had found an innovative way to accommodate special-needs students.

As a concept, this isn't bad. It makes use of a technology that kids are familiar with. It's also a great way to get kids interested and engaged. An iPod is definitely cooler than a big, clunky tape recorder. What good is an assistive technology if the kids won't use it?

The reason I found out about this school at all is that the district wanted permission to have a teacher read the state, high-stakes tests (the *Iowa Tests of Basic Skills*) aloud and record the items on the iPods as a continuation of this use of technology. Their argument was that since the students were accustomed to using it on classroom tests, as per their IEPs, it would be reasonable to record a teacher reading the test battery for the state achievement test as an MP3 file and then give it to the kids on iPods. Unfortunately, there were legal and test security reasons about whether a school was unilaterally creating its own version of the state achievement test. But these evolving technologies are impacting testing all over the country.

ASSISTIVE TECHNOLOGY (AT)

I encourage my students to use "I can" statements in reading class. For example, "I can find the main idea of a story," or "I can independently find a good book to read for sustained silent reading (SSR)." Part of encouraging struggling readers to identify what they can do is to provide opportunities for students to be successful in the classroom. Sometimes, the best way to do this is with technological supports, or AT.

There have been many advances in recent years using technology to help students. Table 3.1 lists some of the more popular AT advancements designed to support literacy instruction. What I have found is that almost ALL of my students benefit from the use of AT. This can be partially explained by **Universal Design for Learning** (UDL). UDL comes from the field of architecture: it is easier to build a house to be compliant with the Americans with Disabilities Act than it is to retrofit the house after it has been built. For instance, a slight slope to the front door, instead of three stairs, makes it more accessible, so that anyone in a wheelchair can live in the house and use the front door. Side benefits of this design are that the walkway is easier to shovel, elderly people who have difficulty climbing stairs can use the walkway easily, and a parent with a stroller can easily roll up to the front door.

UDL has been used to describe instructional practices that are created in response to a student with a specific need, but these practices often have the side benefits of supporting multiple students by offering choice in content, process, or product. For example, if students are given choices for a book project for literature circles, some students may choose to make a movie, perform an interpretive dance, or put on a skit, while others may want to write a traditional book report or write a new ending to the story. By providing choices in product, you are making it possible for students with difficulty writing to do something other than write in the assignment.

In 2007, a Minnesota high school student with dyslexia used *Dragon Naturally Speaking* speech recognition software to take the essay portion of the ACT college entrance test. Permission from ACT to use the device took seven months and the support of an external advocacy group with expertise in the Americans with Disabilities Act. What is significant about this case is that the student had a long history of experience and expertise with AT for writing essays in school, and this case represents a precedent for other students who have accommodations in the classroom that they wish to use for high-stakes tests with security issues.

This is an example of how changing standardized tests leads to a need for new accommodations and how new AT is changing the accommodations requested by special education students for high-stakes tests.

If you are going to write a grant to get AT gadgets in the classroom, there are some inventions made specifically for educational settings that are going to have a huge impact on what happens. It seems as if every year, something new is invented. We are very fortunate at our university to have access to the Iowa Center for Assistive Technology Education and Research (ICATER). Each semester, I bring my class of graduate students to the center to see the latest advances in technology at work. Table 3.1 provides a list of software and tech toys that I've seen used in the classroom to accommodate students with reading and language differences.

This is by no means an exhaustive list. It's just what impressed me the last time I visited the research lab. Hopefully it will inspire you to get on the Internet and see what else is available. Most of these vendors would be happy to send you a free demo kit, especially as new versions of the software are released.

A note about the speech recognition software: don't forget what we talked about at the beginning of this chapter. There is a difference between an accommodation and a modification. If you are concerned with assessing a student's spelling and grammar, then the speech recognition software is probably going to undermine your ability to measure that. It automatically corrects what is spoken into the microphone. But if you are interested in measuring only the content, and mechanics are not part of the score, then by all means, let the students use it! Remember that most of these programs (Dragon Naturally Speaking and Kurzweil 3000) require training to the individual's voice, so don't expect kids to just dive in the first time they turn it on.

Table 3.1 AT for Students to Use in Literacy Assessments

Product	What It Does	Who Should Use It	Suitable for Classroom Assessments	Suitable for High-Stakes, Standardized, Paper-Pencil Tests[a]	Suitable for High-Stakes, Standardized, Computerized Tests[a]
Big Key Keyboard	Just what it says it is—a keyboard with really big keys	Students with small motor control and targeting issues	Yes	No	Yes
Clicker 5	A writing-support tool for any subject area. Build sentences by selecting words, phrases, and pictures; hear words spoken by realistic software speech before you write; and hear completed sentences spoken back	English language learners, students with syntax and pronunciation difficulties	Yes	No	No
Dasher	A software solution for entering text by zooming through letters using a mouse or an eye tracker. Dasher is a keyboardless text entry system that requires only a small movement of the mouse to select letters and characters as they appear on the screen.	Students who can see but who cannot use a keyboard	Yes	No	Yes
Dragon Naturally Speaking	Speech recognition software allows for FAST (upwards of 160 words per minute), continuous (no pauses), large vocabulary (300,000 words) speech. Also allows voice command to control the most recent Windows-based operating systems	Dyslexic and/or learning disabled students	Yes—for writing tests that will not be scored for spelling, but rather on content	Yes—for writing tests	Yes

(Continued)

Table 3.1 (Continued)

Product	What It Does	Who Should Use It	Suitable for Classroom Assessments	Suitable for High-Stakes, Standardized, Paper-Pencil Tests[a]	Suitable for High-Stakes, Standardized, Computerized Tests[a]
Head Mouse Extreme	Replaces the standard computer mouse. The Head Mouse translates natural movements of a users head into directly proportional movements of the computer mouse pointer.	For people who cannot use or have limited use of their hands when controlling a computer or augmentative communication device	Maybe—if the test is computer based	No	Yes
Inspiration	Software that creates graphic organizers to help students organize their thinking	Visual learners	Yes—could help a student organize his or her thoughts for a writing test	No	No
JAWS	This screen reader uses text to speech or Braille display to translate what is on the screen into audio.	Visually impaired and blind users	Yes	No	Yes
Kurzweil 3000	A program that enables conversion of print to electronic text which can be read to the user	Struggling learners, including ELL students and students with special needs	Yes—if the tests are electronic	No	Yes
Livescribe Pulse Pen	Lets the user review written notes that are synchronized with audio. When you tap what you've scribbled or drawn on the special "dot paper" that Pulse works with, you'll hear any audio you recorded while you were writing.	Anyone who would like help remembering what happens in class, teaches note-taking skills	No	No	No
One Handed Keyboard	Just what it says it is—a keyboard with a layout for only one hand	Typists who use only one hand	Maybe—if the student can record responses using a computer	No	Yes

Product	What It Does	Who Should Use It	Suitable for Classroom Assessments	Suitable for High-Stakes, Standardized, Paper-Pencil Tests[a]	Suitable for High-Stakes, Standardized, Computerized Tests[a]
Read and Write Gold	Text to speech software	Visually impaired and blind users	Yes—tests can be scanned so the software can read the text aloud to the user	No	Yes
Softype Onscreen Keyboard	An on-screen keyboard which replaces a standard keyboard with a full featured on-screen keyboard enabling text input into Windows applications	Students using a Head Mouse can dwell on the keys of the on-screen keyboard to type	Yes	No	No
SpeakQ	Allows a user to write while speaking continuously	Students with learning disabilities could benefit from word prediction and text-to-speech functions	Yes	No	Yes
Window Eyes	Screen reader software that converts text to synthesized speech. Portable and can run on a flash drive, which makes it easy for students to take from home to class	Visually impaired or blind students who need access to Excel, Word, PowerPoint, and Outlook	Yes	No	Yes
WordQ	Word prediction and text-to-speech software. When you type a letter, WordQ predicts what you might want to write and displays a list of correctly spelled words from which you can choose. When you see the word you want, you can choose it with a single keystroke or with the mouse.	English language learners (ELLs), students with learning disabilities	Yes	No	No
ZoomText	A text magnifier and reader	Visually impaired and blind users	Yes	Yes	Yes

a. Many of these devices and programs require a great deal of practice before a student becomes proficient. Even if the use of the device is written into the child's IEP, do not assume that (a) it will be allowed to be used on the state test or (b) that the device will not inadvertently become an obstacle to the child in a high-stakes testing situation if he or she is not completely comfortable and independent with the AT.

RESPONSE TO INTERVENTION (RTI)

The Individuals with Disabilities Education Improvement Act (IDEIA) was reauthorized in 2004 to reflect new ideas about learning disabilities. The new IDEIA eliminated the requirement that students must exhibit a severe discrepancy between intellectual ability and achievement in order to be found eligible for special education and related services as a student with a learning disability. Now, for students to be considered for special education services based on a learning disability, first, they must have been provided with effective instruction, and then their progress must have been measured through data-based documentation of repeated assessments of achievement. With RTI, schools identify students at risk for poor learning outcomes, identify students with learning disabilities, monitor student progress, provide evidence-based interventions, and adjust the intensity and nature of those interventions depending on a student's responsiveness. RTI is an educational process that evaluates how well students respond to academic instruction and then uses those student responses to guide educational decisions in three phases, typically known as tiers:

Tier 1: Allows for differentiated instruction of the regular education curriculum.

Tier 2: Scaffolded interventions are provided to struggling students in the general education classroom setting.

Tier 3: More intensive interventions and special education services are provided.

The kinds of differentiated instruction used in RTI include frequent monitoring of student learning through diagnostic and formative assessments and immediate interventions, often with the use of technology and intensive one-on-one instruction. Do not be surprised to learn that RTI looks different across school contexts. For more information about RTI, check out www.rti4success.org.

DIFFERENTIATED INSTRUCTION (DI)

The interventions in language and literacy that are called for by RTI include using classroom assessment information to differentiate, or change, the way struggling readers are taught. When RTI is implemented properly, teachers use research-based practices to teach, monitor student progress with formative assessments, and then modify and adjust instruction to make sure students are learning.

One of the most important assumptions of differentiated instruction is that all students can learn. With this in mind, teachers look for appropriate early interventions to support struggling readers. The best way to make sure the instructional interventions are working is to collaborate with the special education teachers and other faculty on the students' IEPs. The collaborative process might look like this (see Figure 3.1):

Step 1: Define the problem. What specifically is the student's reading issue? What assessment data support your diagnosis?

Step 2: Plan on differentiated instruction for the students. Bearing in mind the student's strengths and weaknesses, develop lesson plans to re-teach and make instructional adjustments.

Step 3: Use additional assessment data to evaluate the student's progress. This is where formative assessment techniques come in (see Chapter 2). This is an iterative process. That is, it is an intentional problem-solving process designed to repeat.

Differentiating instruction is particularly important at the high school level. When a student enters the classroom reading at a second-grade level, your strategies for teaching don't need to be completely changed because of the age of the student. For example, I have a colleague who has created

Figure 3.1 Intervention–Evaluation Cycle

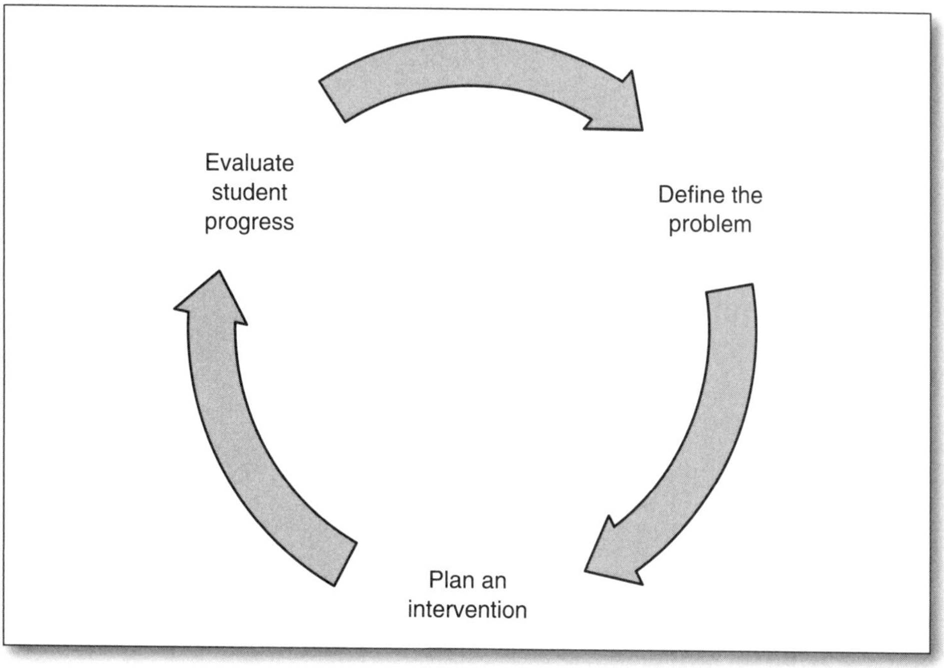

three centers in her high school reading recovery class. When students enter, they begin at one of the three centers and switch after 15 minutes until they have been in all three during the 45-minute class period. In one center, the students are reading self-selected books independently and answering questions about what they have read in a journal notebook. In another, the students are wearing headphones and working on the computer at their own level, using the Scholastic Read 180 software with leveled reading activities that advance as the student's ability progresses. In the third center, the teacher is asking students to take turns reading a newspaper article aloud and targeting questions to the small group about genre and text format. When older students come to the classroom with a wide range of abilities, it is imperative to provide a variety of learning experiences and a range of activities that can be adjusted to fit any reading level.

ENGLISH LANGUAGE LEARNERS (ELLs)

Just as there is a separate set of rules and regulations guiding the testing of special education students, there are also special rules for nonnative speakers of English. NCLB requires schools that receive Title I funding to assess the level of English Language Proficiency (ELP) in students who are labeled as English language learners (ELLs). You may be surprised to know that each state has its own definitions for who qualifies as an ELL. Methods used to determine a student's status include home language surveys and English language proficiency tests (Abedi, 2008). Sometimes, a new student might come to you with an ELL designation from his or her last school, but the student won't qualify for ELL services in your school because the qualifications are different.

Many tests provide a separate set of norms for assessing culturally and linguistically diverse students (Rhodes, Ochoa, & Ortiz, 2005). These might take the form of Spanish translations of a test or a special set of norms to compare the scores of your ELLs to other ELL kids who took the same test.

There are also instruments, such as the Qualitative Use of English and Spanish Tasks (QUEST) (Gonzalez, Brusca-Vega, & Yawkey, 1996) that can be used to measure cultural and linguistic differences in children and separate those from mild disabilities. Nonverbal tests (tests without words) are good ways to see how children think about concepts with language, whatever the language, and are probably the best ways to identify gifted and talented ELLs (Lohman, Korb, & Lakin, 2008).

Remember, there is no one right way to teach any group of people how to read. All of this is contextual, and it depends on your students' individual needs, your school climate, and the support you have from parents and the larger community. That is why great teaching is an art. As the artist, it's your job to collect the supplies and tools you will need to create a classroom of readers.

END-OF-CHAPTER QUIZ

Joe, one of your eleventh-grade gifted students, has dislocated his shoulder surfing while vacationing on a cruise with his family. He has lost the use of his right arm for at least six weeks while he heals from the resulting surgery. Unfortunately, the social studies exams, due at the end of the course, require that Surfer Joe has to write five pages in class next Wednesday. Joe has seen some of the special education kids in your class using the Dragon Naturally Speaking software and would like permission to dictate his social studies test into the computer. What do you do?

1. Dragon Naturally Speaking requires training. Let him borrow one of the laptops over the weekend to get the software to recognize his voice and see how he does. It might not work very well, since he is a new user, but Joe is smart, so maybe it won't matter.

2. Issue Joe a scribe. One of the school secretaries can type while he talks.

3. Have him write with his left hand.

4. Let him give his answers orally instead.

4 Attitude and Motivation

Chapter Highlights

- Review of research on what motivates people
- The difference between preparation and motivation
- Why pizza parties don't raise test scores
- Teaching tip: Use reading tests as a genre
- Involving families with parent/teacher/student conferences

I have a poster in my classroom that says, "Attitude is the mind's paint-brush: It can color any situation." Likewise, the teacher's attitude is going to color the entire classroom. If teachers and students decide to regard the testing program as an extra burden, then most of its potential value as a tool for instructional feedback will be lost. Chapter 4 reviews the research on the relationship between attitude and motivation and the ways we can encourage students to do their best on the high-stakes reading tests without the use of incentives, bribery, or coercion. The chapter also includes teaching ideas for approaching the reading test format as a genre in and of itself, which is a way to reduce test anxiety in students.

Good tests can contribute to the effectiveness of teaching when the test score reports are specific and detailed enough to guide individualized instruction. Regardless of what time of year your school conducts tests, the score reports from the year before should be reviewed by teachers and guidance counselors in the fall prior to the start of the school year. From these score reports, you can begin to develop an educational profile of the incoming students. The next step is the important part that many schools miss: from here, an informal conversation should be held with each of the students about what you see as their school-based strengths and weaknesses based on not only their test scores but also their grades from the year before and what you may have observed after a few weeks of school. The goal of these conversations should be to build up feelings of confidence, not to make comments that might make students anxious. Then with the standardized state test scores in front of the student, lead a conversation about the nature and purposes of the tests and how testing information is used by teachers to inform instruction, particularly differentiated instruction. Figure 4.1 shows a sample Student Interview Sheet. In this way, you are not only including students in their educational decision-making process; you are also demystifying how the test scores and grades factor into an overall academic profile of the student. The final part of the student interview sheet, setting academic goals for the year, is perhaps the most important motivational tool in your tool chest. But before we talk about goal setting, let's review other motivational practices your principal might already have started to implement.

The No Child Left Behind (NCLB) legislation of 2001 has generated unprecedented pressure among school administrators to do whatever it takes to raise the reading, math, and science test scores of their students. Because principals are taught that part of being a transformational leader is creating a particular culture in a school, it stands to reason the role of cheerleader and head motivator might fall to a school principal interested in exciting a student body to a particular task, like taking the NCLB tests. What is more, the principal is the first person to fall victim to state-sponsored sanctions like reorganization if the school consistently fails to make **adequate yearly progress (AYP).** According to the program evaluation of NCLB conducted by the federal Department of Education, "Appointment of a new principal, although not specified as a restructuring intervention under NCLB, was reported by 20 percent of schools in restructuring status, as well as by 20 to 21 percent of schools in other stages of school improvement status" (U.S. Department of Education, 2007). So school principals, despite the limited instructional interaction they may have with students, have reason to concern themselves with raising student test scores.

Due to the incredible pressure administrators find themselves under to impact the test scores, some of the strangest changes are being implemented in schools across the country: pep rallies, pizza parties, cheers and songs about the state test, offers of days off from school for increased student test scores, and—what I consider to be the weirdest yet—bonus pay to teachers whose students get higher scores. Figure 4.2 shows the four models for performance pay that have evolved in the United States in the past five years.

Figure 4.1   Sample Worksheet to Use With Students at the Beginning of the Year

Student Interview Sheet

Student Name: _____

Test Scores from Last Year: Reading _____ Math _____ Science _____

End of Last Year's Grades:

Language Arts _____

Mathematics   _____

Science   _____

Social Studies _____

Student's Favorite Subject:

Hobbies Outside of School:

Academic Strengths (based on test scores, grades, teacher observation):

Academic Goals for this year:

Figure 4.2 Misguided Motivation Methods

Pay for Performance Models

Merit pay: Individual teachers receive bonuses based on improvements in their performance or increased responsibilities, as measured by senior faculty and/or administrators.

Knowledge- and skills-based pay: Teachers earn permanent salary increases for acquiring new skills (inservices or graduate classes) and applying those skills to their practice.

Performance pay: Salary increases are tied to improvements in students' performance measured by standardized tests or other criteria.

School-based performance pay: All professional staff in a school earn a bonus if students meet particular goals.

Just to put this in perspective, you could offer me a trip to Paris if I could pass the AP calculus test. But the fact of the matter is, if I haven't the first clue how to do the calculus items on the test, it really isn't a question of motivation, is it? I need someone to teach me how to solve the problems that are going to be on the test.

For the last two years, my school has had a "Testing Pep Rally" in order to motivate students before testing starts. I find this problematic on a couple of levels. First, it takes up an hour of instructional time during the days leading directly to the test. In that amount of time, I personally can think of half a dozen reading strategies we could review using an engaging text. My second problem (and I suspect I'm not the only teacher frustrated by this) with the "pep rally" is that it has ended up being nothing more than a time to get our students totally riled up and out of control. The first year, the high school peer leaders and band came. They changed the words from some of the yells the high school uses to incorporate our school name and the state test. This took approximately 4 minutes of the hour. The rest of the time was a relay race between the grades at our school with everyone in the stands either yelling or sitting there bored.

From the beginning of the year, I let my students know that luck plays little part in school. They don't need to worry about the big projects they have heard fifth graders have to do, or the dreaded test. I can confidently assure them that we will be ready by the time of the test. Before each testing session, I make my students turn to their neighbor and remind them of certain things. They repeat after me words of advice to their neighbor, such as "Don't forget to use the multiple-choice strategy," and in writing,

"Don't forget a topic and conclusion." No matter what words of advice I have my students give each other, I always end it the same way, "Good luck, but you don't need it, because you've got skill." My students don't need luck or a pep rally to motivate them. They are ready, and they have been taught what they need to know. I think it empowers my students to know they are in charge of their testing. They will not encounter random information in the test booklet. This is what we've been doing *all* year!

I totally appreciate the desperation school principals may feel. If their school is not making AYP, then they are in danger of losing their jobs. Unfortunately, the activities they seem to be gravitating toward are not grounded in any sort of motivation research. Instead, the selected activities seem to stem from a sports coaching model. As much as I can gather, the line of thinking goes something like this: cheerleaders and pep rallies are used to motivate the football team before a big game, right? So why don't we use the same strategies to motivate the kids to do better on the big test!

Let's take a quick look at motivation research and see why this is not a good idea.

MOTIVATION RESEARCH

Theories of Motivation

Behavioral and cognitive theories of motivation are sometimes applied by educators searching for ways to encourage students to be better test takers, especially in schools where student performance is lower than expected based on other indicators. Advocates argue incentives will create an environment where students take learning seriously, resulting in greater effort. These incentives in practice range from punishments—for example, grade retention—to rewards—like days off from school. Behaviorists argue for the use of punishments and rewards (both intrinsic and extrinsic) as ways to entice students into learning: for instance, paying students in cash for their performance on tests.

Research tells us that engaged reading is absolutely related to reading achievement (Guthrie & Wigfield, 2000). When children are reading independently, for their own purposes and for enjoyment, their ability to comprehend texts in general increases. But student attitudes vary from day to day. Over time, how do we keep student motivation high no matter what the reading assignment?

Cognitive motivation research suggests that students should set goals for learning and children should be taught to attribute their success or failure to particular behaviors. For example, drawing from the research on reducing test anxiety, some schools have worked with students to develop strategies for coping with testing situations, such as time management or desensitization (Schunk, Pintrich, & Meece, 2008, pp. 228–233). We apply this concept to the reading and language forms we use in the classroom. After each writing prompt or assessment, students look at specific areas to work on and then set goals for performance on the next assessment.

In my classroom, I have tried a variety of methods to motivate students to read independently. Recently, one method that has been very successful is one I dubbed "The Great Genre Challenge." At the beginning of the year, I introduce the students to the ten different genres I want them to read and know during their year with me: poetry, biography, autobiography, traditional literature, informational, historical fiction, realistic fiction, fantasy, science fiction, and mystery. My classroom library is organized by these genres in color-coded tubs, and there are posters in the reading area to remind the students of the characteristics of each genre.

Once the students are familiar with the different genres and the check-out system of the classroom library, I issue the challenge. I challenge my students to read 250 books of a variety of genres. They work together as a class, and we keep track of the books read by a color-coded paper chain strung across the window. Students also have an individual reading log that I can pull out and conference with students about their own reading, but as a class, all we have to do is look at the paper chain and see that no one has read a poetry book in several weeks. Should we get some additional poetry books from the public library to supplement our collection? After the initial challenge is met and we've read 250 books, we challenge another class to the same goal: Read another 250 books.

What was the prize for my students? No pizza parties or movies or anything like that. The class that gets to 250 first gets *bragging rights*. Kids tend to get so into the competition that they are finding the genres they love, recommending books to their peers, and encouraging one another to keep reading. Even if my class doesn't win, no one loses! I have hooked my students on reading. That is something that will be rewarding to them long after the pizza boxes have been thrown out or some cheap toy from the discount store broken or lost.

Test Anxiety

Test anxiety is one of the behaviors associated with affect and motivation in test taking.

Harlen and Crick (2003, p. 34) write that the pressure of higher stakes on the tests is directly related to the level of test anxiety. Cizek and Burg (2006) add that anxiety has effects on motivation both overall and on specific tests with future consequences; researchers have noted that test anxiety is sometimes inversely related to academic performance (Paulsen & Feldman, 1999). Ideally, test takers should be motivated to do their best on the summative NCLB achievement tests, and their anxiety about the high stakes of the test should not be so great that it interferes with the students' ability to perform to the best of their abilities. Students with test anxiety see evaluation situations as threatening, which is further enforced when in future test settings, their anxiety lowers their performance and thus confirms their threat of evaluation (Cizek & Burg, 2006).

In addition to helping students develop coping strategies to deal with test anxiety, schools also attempt to provide calming and supportive test environments. They do this by providing students with breaks in testing, relaxation techniques, and test-taking strategies (Cizek & Burg, 2006). Familiarization with the tests in the form of test preparation activities has also been a strategy teachers have used to reduce test anxiety.

In order to instill more confidence in my students, I am very serious about keeping my own attitude in check during testing time. I want my kids to understand they are more than ready for the test, and having a teacher with an attitude that shows this can help a great deal. This test is nothing out of the ordinary. It is not some magic booklet that is going to present concepts they have never seen before. It is a part of school that ensures we've all been doing what we're supposed to do—that the teachers have been teaching effectively, and the students have been learning. Well, we have!

One thing that is difficult to control is trying to shelter my students from the stressed out, frazzled attitudes of administrators and other teachers. For example, last year during the state test with the acronym "PAWS," Proficiency Assessments for Wyoming Students. I found some cute bandanas with paw prints all over them. I purchased one for each of my students to wear while we tested, just a fun, relaxing start to our month of testing. Each day that we tested students would take out the bandana and try to come up with unique ways to display them. It was fun, and it was my way of reminding the students that the test was NOT something to be scared of. Well one day some students forgot to remove their bandanas before recess and were reprimanded by another staff member for wearing the bandanas, saying that they were gang paraphernalia. I expected my students to be upset, and I apologized for not reminding them to take the bandanas off before they left the room. They didn't seem to mind; they were only curious why the adults in the building had been so stressed out lately. I felt that I had accomplished my goal of creating a calm, testing environment.

INCENTIVES

There is a debate in the educational psychology literature about not only what types of external incentives are effective in motivating students but also when it is most effective to deliver the rewards in order to increase a student's intrinsic motivation. A meta-analysis of 128 studies about rewards and motivation (Deci, Koestner, & Ryan, 1999) suggested that "tangible rewards tend to have a substantially negative effect on intrinsic motivation" (p. 659). So while rewards may have the short-term effect of changing behavior, the long-term effects can lead people to not take responsibility for motivating themselves. In an educational setting where the goal is to create a lifelong love of learning, the findings of this research might give cause for alarm.

In contrast, a meta-analysis of ninety-six studies about rewards conducted by a different research team (Cameron & Pierce, 1994) found rewards have a negative impact on intrinsic motivation only when the reward is offered "without consideration of any standard of performance" (p. 397). In other words, so long as a reward is contingent on performance, the intrinsic motivation will be unaffected. Given these research results, rewards to students for success in academic endeavors should not impact a student's drive to learn for personal reasons. Further work suggests the efficacy of an incentive program is related to the difficulty of the tasks. When the tasks become increasingly challenging, rewards can be used to increase task persistence (Cameron, Pierce, Banko, & Gear, 2005).

Given these conflicting results in the motivation literature, it is no wonder educators are left with some confusion about the most effective ways to use rewards and incentives as tools to motivate reluctant students. The use of punishments and rewards have been used in schools to entice students into learning, with *A*'s, gold stars, and even paying students in cash for their performance on tests (Kohn, 1993/1999). But such strategies seem to reward just the outcome of assessments, not necessarily the learning itself. Intrinsic motivation theories posit student engagement is highest when students value the task for its interest or for its relevance to a future goal (Roderick & Engel, 2001). Extrinsic motivation involves the use of rewards and threats to encourage students to desire to attain an external goal (Donald, 1999). However, these distinctions are not necessarily mutually exclusive and probably subject to individual interpretation by the student. For example, grades and test scores are often used by teachers to emphasize normative, social comparisons and to incentivize achievement behaviors (Ames, 1992). If a student believes good grades are necessary to attain a personal goal, then it might stand to reason that for that particular student, the motivation is intrinsic.

GOAL SETTING

Cognitive theorists believe patterns of thought and behavior can be taught with activities like goal setting, and test anxiety can be managed with cognitive therapies. Locke and Latham (2002) summarized thirty-five years of empirical research on goal setting theory and found "goal-setting theory is among the most valid and practical theories of employee motivation in organizational psychology" (p. 714). When applied to educational settings, cognitive motivation theories suggest students should set goals for learning and children should be explicitly taught to attribute their success or failure to particular behaviors.

As a way to make all classroom testing meaningful, I always let students know what the test will be used for. After I administer a test reading a single story, I let the students know I will use their results to determine what groups I will pull back during differentiated reading group time. For larger tests, like our theme tests, which we use to determine proficiency on grade-level standards, I let the students know we look at these results for placement in after school, summer school, and sixth-grade language/reading class placement. The same is true for the results of our state test. I explain to them that I will use the results to make instructional decisions and to help the students measure their academic progress.

If having fun and making friends is a more important goal for a student than getting an *A*, you need to be prepared to have a conversation with that student about ways you will honor that, within the context of your own goals for the class. You can explain that the students will have opportunities for book clubs and group literacy work. Make your curricular methods visible to the students so they can appreciate that you are consciously crafting an environment in your classroom where kids will learn to love to read—based in part on their stated goals.

But the goals that are set need to be attainable. Let me tell you a story about my guitar lessons.

So I'm not a very good guitar player. I am taking lessons from Seth, who did not have the heart to tell me that the music I was bringing in (the transcribed tablature music from Eric Clapton *Unplugged*) was too hard for me. Instead, for at least a month, I muddled through a couple of songs never finding any success. Disheartened, I gave up. Then, finding his teacher voice, Seth suggested instead a much easier guitar book of Beatles music, complete with strumming patterns and chords drawn out. Suddenly, I was not only able to play the songs, but what I was playing was actually recognizable to the people in my family who were forced to listen to me practice.

My point is this: set attainable, realistic goals with your students, and don't be afraid to ratchet the goals down a notch to be sure your students have a fair shot at success. When a struggling second-grade reader comes to you with *Harry Potter* and declares that he or she wants to read it for sustained silent reading (SSR), it is really tempting to encourage him or her to try. But what is the outcome if you set up your students for failure? Like me, they will have a hard time maintaining the motivation to keep trying if every attempt they make is met with failure. You don't have to crush your struggling reader's excitement about *Harry Potter*, just as Seth didn't discourage me with Eric Clapton. Just be ready with an alternative that in your expert opinion is more attainable and within the same genre, thereby setting your students up for success. One alternative would be to present the student with another fantasy that is at the student's reading level. Or perhaps you have a reading station set up at one of your centers. If this student is not the only person in the class interested in reading this book, then that can become a listening center. Another idea would be to involve the parents and have them read the book with their child either together before bedtime or get the book on CD to listen to it in the car, as the family runs around town.

One of the ways we apply technology to motivate students is the use of MP3 book packets. Students can check out a packet from the library that has a book and an MP3 player with the book recorded on it. The MP3 is locked and can't be erased or added to. This allows struggling readers to access grade-level materials that they haven't been able to read independently. This alleviates a common problem for struggling readers at the intermediate- and middle-school levels where the books at the students' interest levels are not at the students' independent reading levels. Of course, this does affect what skills and strategies the student is applying; they are listening rather than just reading. But I talk to my students who have the MP3's checked out to make certain they are doing what good readers do: predict, infer, clarify, monitor, evaluate, summarize, question, understand cause/effect, and story structure—and the list goes on and on. It just takes the *word attack* strategy out of the equation for these struggling readers.

Engaged readers are motivated readers (Verhoeven & Snow, 2001, p. 159). Chapter 5 describes ways to connect units of study to real-world contexts to make reading relevant. More important, the texts teachers select for instructional purposes need to be interesting and support students' self-expression. In other words, the texts need to be culturally and socially relevant to them. Unfortunately, test preparation curriculums often, ironically, have the opposite effect on students. Since the literature selected for reading tests is chosen for different reasons and serves different purposes than the literature selected by teachers for instruction, it should come as no surprise that students often do not feel connected, engaged, or motivated by test preparation materials. When this is the case, it can be detrimental to student performance, causing students to perform lower than their actual ability.

I wanted to know what kinds of motivation and preparation techniques were being used across a Midwestern state. With a team of research assistants, I called one hundred principals (a random, stratified sample) and asked them what they were doing to prepare and motivate their students (Hollingworth, Dude, & Shepherd, 2010). Sixty-three percent of the principals reported using activities as rewards for students whose test scores went up from the previous year. These activities ranged from pizza parties to field trips to days off from school. When we asked them, as follow up, what evidence they had that these strategies were working, most principals could not point to any specific data. The test scores were not going up because of the reward activities.

My favorite comment was the principal who said that before he started working at his school a year ago, they used to give kids a day off if their test scores went up. When I asked him why he eliminated that practice when he took over, he answered, "Because this isn't a prison."

WHAT TO DO IF YOUR PRINCIPAL WANTS TO USE PIZZA PARTIES TO BRIBE STUDENTS

When we asked principals what evidence they had that the strategies they were using to motivate students to succeed on the state tests were working, most of them gave me blank looks.

The one good answer I did receive came from a high school principal who said that morale had gotten so bad in his school during testing that kids had started misbehaving or faking illness during the test so they could go to the office. Once an ice cream party was offered to students who were observed by their homeroom teacher as doing their personal best, the referrals to the office during testing dropped to only one student. That was his evidence that the motivation strategies were working. Bribery for behavior isn't the same as increasing achievement.

If you are in a school where the principal wants to implement a motivational prize program to kids for their achievement on a high-stakes test, ask what evidence will be used to measure the efficacy of the new practice and what the research base is to support the new strategy. It is understandable that the school principals want to effect a positive climate at the school. Of course, a positive attitude is going to affect a student taking a high-stakes test. What has caused your principal to come to the conclusion that motivation is the root cause of the test scores in your school? What if it's something bigger—such as the students needing to learn the skills that are going to be measured on the test?

I also recommend that you and your colleagues read Alfie Kohn's book *Punished by Rewards: The Trouble With Gold Stars, Incentive Plans, A's, Praise, and Other Bribes* (Kohn, 1999). It's the kind of book that would be good to discuss in a faculty book club, because you will find so many real-life examples in it about ways we inadvertently undermine our students' natural curiosity and motivation with artificial reward structures.

Now you might say, "This is great to warn teachers to get educated and be ready to fight; however, there are many districts where it doesn't matter what teachers think—namely, in my district." In that case, remember that you and your class will participate in whatever incentive programs are being offered because it is mandatory, but you still have to know how to introduce the programs to your room. Your students have to know that as their teacher, you believe in their ability to perform well on the test. They must also know that their best is expected regardless of any incentive program being offered. In a sense, you have to make your students realize that the incentives are silly. Of course, they will not perform better on a test because a pizza party or pajama party is on the line. They are going to perform well because they are well prepared.

Remember, your students don't need luck on any exam, because you have been preparing for the tests and they have all the skills they will need. Do not just rely on the promise of pizza to hope your students perform well. A teacher has to know that her students will perform well because they have been prepared well. And, if they get a free pizza lunch at the end, so be it.

THE USE OF PRACTICE TESTS: PREPARATION OR MOTIVATION?

We found that 39 percent of the principals in our study had initiated a test preparation program in their schools. Many of these programs included practice tests. On the state department of education website, many states release test items from old tests in the form of practice tests. Several publishing companies sell practice tests for classroom use that consist of *mocked* items, as opposed to released items from previous tests. These are items that look just like the ones that are on the high-stakes tests, but a few details are changed so that the item is not an exact version of the test. Part of making sure that your students feel comfortable with the test format is giving them a chance to see what the test is going to look like ahead of time. By all means, give the kids a chance to see what the item format looks like so they don't inadvertently become confused by the directions or by the item type. But everything in moderation: if you spend too much of your class time practicing test items, you might not get around to actually teaching the kids how to read. Personally, I start teaching test-taking strategies from the very first test we take in September. We go over multiple-choice strategies and discuss how to read and react to constructed or extended response answers. By introducing this early in the year and revisiting it each time we take a test, I have taken away any feelings of uncertainty about reading a test or knowing what different key words in a question mean. If a question asks students to compare and contrast, my students have seen this before. We have highlighted those key words and worked together on how to best address those key words. This way, by the time the official state test rolls around in the spring, my kids are ready to go.

Remember: your job is to create a culture in the classroom that fosters students' intrinsic motivation to practice authentic, everyday literacies.

TEST PREPARATION: ANALYZING TESTS AS A READING GENRE

A comprehensive K–12 reading curriculum prepares students for the myriad of genres they will encounter as they embark on the journey toward becoming lifelong readers: everything from digital media, magazines, and newspapers to bus schedules, cookbooks, best-selling novels, and how-to manuals with highly technical, specialized vocabulary. As children travel along the path toward lifelong literacy, they will experience all kinds of real-world reading, both in and out of school settings. However, successful students are also able to master the types of literacy tasks that are privileged in American school curriculums. These are reading tasks that are typically reflected in the tests that are used to make high-stakes decisions about students, teachers, and schools. As such, schools have a responsibility to prepare test takers for this kind of specialized reading and to extract information that is both explicitly and implicitly presented in the text. This is not to suggest the replacement of excellent, research-based reading programs grounded in real-world literacy with a test preparation curriculum. Rather, this is an approach to teaching the skills needed to successfully attack reading tests using the specialized skills specific to this particular genre. The purpose of this approach is threefold: to demystify reading comprehension tests for students, to teach the skills good readers need to extract information (reading to learn), and to construct meaning from the reading comprehension tests themselves.

The reading passages that are chosen for high-stakes, multiple-choice tests are selected for their obscurity so that the materials are unknown to all test takers. Otherwise, students who might previously have seen the passages would be privileged in the test taking. The kind of reading that is done on standardized tests is a genre all its own: abbreviated reading selections taken out of context with questions in either a multiple choice or an open-ended format. Since this is not the kind of literacy activity most adults engage in once they are out of school, it is not reasonable to expect that preparation for this reading genre should supplant a comprehensive reading curriculum. But it is completely reasonable to find ways to give students the tools they need to read novel texts for facts, generalizations, and inferences while preparing them for the format and structure of test questions.

An effective strategy for preparing students to take reading tests is to familiarize them with the types of passages that are selected by test developers to appear in a reading test. This familiarization serves a dual purpose: test takers who typically experience test anxiety will be comforted by knowing more about the tests, and students who need extra practice reading a variety of unfamiliar texts for information can get that experience.

Many states, like Texas, release old forms of the assessments used for accountability purposes on the state department of education website. Each reading test used by the states for high-stakes decisions asks questions based on at least one poem, a piece of fiction, and a selection of nonfiction text. After carefully examining a few samples of the kinds of passages that are on these tests, students will be able to identify some of the common features of these reading selections.

Here are five teaching activities that position reading tests as a genre of study. These ideas can get you started as you build your collection of lesson plans:

1. Download a copy of the most recent version of your state's reading test and print each reading passage on a different page. Break your class into small groups of three or four students, and provide each group with one of the reading passages you have printed. Ask students to count the number of words in the passages on the tests. Many states use test specifications that explicitly state the number of words (commonly either 250 or 700) to appear in each passage. Then, have students pretend to be test developers and choose an excerpt from the nonfiction text in their social studies or science textbook and edit it to the required number of words without losing

the main idea of the passage. This activity lets students see how hard it is to edit a passage without losing the author's meaning, and it also requires students to read in the content areas for a new purpose. This is also a new way for them to develop an understanding of finding the main idea.

2. There is usually a section of nonfiction about something obscure, like the history of umbrellas, which rarely any child in the age group being tested has been exposed to in advance of reading the passage. Ask your students to think about *why* a passage like this might be chosen for a test. Discuss the idea that the best way to test a reader's ability to read and to learn is to provide the test taker with information about a topic where the only information the student has access to comes from the passage itself, and not from past experience. Have the class brainstorm a list of unusual ideas that might make good testing fodder and have them look up those topics on the internet, looking for passages online to share with the class. This would be a great homework assignment if your students have access to the Internet at home. If not, it could also be done during computer lab time. If doing this during computer lab time, it might be effective to have the students work in pairs and then share their findings with the class. One of the problems the students will quickly discover is how difficult it is to pay attention to a topic that does not hold the reader's interest. This can lead to a fruitful conversation about the process of writing nonfiction in a way that both informs and entertains. As a first step toward item writing, groups of students could decide together, and highlight, the portions of the passages selected by the class as question worthy. For instance, the parts of a reading selection that explain how to do something usually result in a question for the reader about what should happen next. So this activity can scaffold for students the process of test development where the topic has been selected and the reading passage itself is subjected to scrutiny for item fertility. In other words, does the selected passage have enough content (is it fertile enough), to generate lots of good questions?

3. The pieces chosen for tests are either original pieces created specifically for the test, or they are taken from an obscure book that students normally don't select to read for pleasure. This is a purposeful decision by test developers so that students who might be lucky enough to have studied the passage in advance of the test won't have an unfair advantage over kids who are seeing it for the first time. Challenge your students to visit the public library or a garage

sale and bring in a book that nobody in the class has ever seen before. The book has to be written for children, and it has to have a section that can be excerpted. The purpose of this exercise is to get students talking about what kinds of reading are typical for people their age and what kinds are atypical. Be prepared to make a chart comparing what students choose to read in class during free reading (SSR, sustained silent reading, or DEAR, drop everything and read) and how it compares with the obscure selections people brought in for this exercise.

4. The fiction pieces selected for standardized tests usually include either an interesting character or a particularly colorful use of language. There will be questions about those sections of the passage. Using either the passages your students selected from Activity 3, or from a short story you chose, have the students predict what parts of the passage might be ripe for test items. Ask your students to write their own test questions from the passages as a strategy for taking the mystery out of the test development process, and to help them better understand these types of test questions. The questions the students write should model the kinds of items that appear in the standardized tests given in your state. For instance, some state reading tests have a blend of open-ended as well as multiple-choice items. After they have written the items, have them trade with each other and try to take the tests written by their peers.

5. To prepare for the piece of poetry that will inevitably be on the test, ask your students to consider music as poetry. Have them choose the lyrics from their favorite song and analyze the lyrics as if they were a poem, looking for alliteration, prosody (the meter, rhythm, and intonation of a poem), metaphors, and other grade-level appropriate literary elements that align with the curriculum. If the lyrics a student selects lack ample literary devices to warrant an analysis, discuss this and ask the student to choose a different song. One of the more interesting effects of this activity is that it requires students to think critically about the music they listen to everyday. Then, ask the students to write a series of multiple-choice questions about the lyrics. This is a higher-order-thinking activity because in order to write the questions, the students need to know and to be able to apply the parts of a poem and the meaning of the literary terms.

Again, these activities are not meant to replace a thoughtful, comprehensive reading program grounded in research on best practices. Rather, they are meant to be treated as an approach to reading test preparation that goes beyond practice tests. When reading comprehension tests are positioned as a genre to study, not only are the tests themselves demystified, but test takers are armed with strategies for successfully navigating the kinds of reading that are presented in standardized assessments.

For other ideas on treating reading tests as a genre study, see Hornof's article in *The Reading Teacher*, "Reading Tests as a Genre Study" (2008) and Fuhrken's (2009) book, *What Every Elementary Teacher Needs To Know About Reading Tests From Someone Who Has Written Them*.

COMMUNICATION WITH STAKEHOLDERS

I can't say enough about the value of parent-teacher-student conferences. What better way to engage students in their education than to let them lead a conversation with their parents about their academic strengths, weaknesses, and their points of pride and growth? Family conferences like this are also an excellent way to send the message to your class parents that you view them as valuable partners in the education of their children.

Some tests provide score reports that allow users to plot their growth from year to year. It is especially helpful if the growth is expressed in terms of grade-level equivalents (as opposed to a standard **scale score**, for example), so that parents and students can see whether or not a year's worth of growth is being achieved from year to year. Make sure the test results are meaningful to the learners, let the students themselves lead the conference with their parents, and have them explain the ways they see their talents reflected (or not!) in the test results. By using test results in this way and having students take ownership of their scores, they will find that tests are more meaningful. Too often, tests are given and then shipped off to be scored, without follow-up. Then the next time the students hear about testing is in the subsequent grade. Also, by allowing students to evaluate how the test did not fully measure their talents or abilities, it will empower them to see that the test is not some big, scary looming event to get through at the end of the year.

END-OF-CHAPTER QUIZ

Your principal decides to read Hooray for Diffendoofer Day *by Dr. Seuss (published posthumously with help from Jack Prelutsky and Lane Smith) to the entire middle school in a special assembly to excite the students to do their best on the state test. This is a story about a school with creative teachers and a nervous principal who worries the school will be closed if the students fail a standardized test. At the end, the principal is happy to announce that all of the students passed because the teachers had taught the children to think, and he rewards the school with a party with "pizza, milk, and cake." After the assembly, the principal wants every teacher to lead a class discussion of the book and to find the ways the teachers in your school are like the teachers in the Diffendoofer School.*

What do you do?

1. Go to the assembly and then give the kids free time or study hall when you get back to the room. Middle schoolers are going to think this is the dumbest thing they ever heard. There will be a full-scale revolt if you try to lead some lame conversation about innovative teaching from a Dr. Seuss book.

2. Get the kids pizza, milk, and cake to have after the story is read.

3. Go online and download activities to go with *Hooray for Diffendoofer Day* and try to make a lesson plan out of it. Maybe there is music to go with the song in the book.

4. Privately ask the principal what he hopes to gain from this exercise and how it fits with current research on motivation. Try to talk him out of it.

5. Insist that the principal develop a procedure for measuring the effectiveness of this motivation strategy so that it can be evaluated for its usefulness for next year.

5 Engaged Independent Reading

Chapter Highlights

- Why real-world reading experiences are important
- Providing real-world reading experiences for your students
- Boy versus girl readers
- Implementing book clubs

Real readers read real books and select books about topics that are interesting to them. The most effective and memorable moments in school happen when students are actively engaged as learners and can see the connections between what they are doing and the world outside the classroom. When the curriculum is narrowed down to test-preparation worksheets and skills and drills, teachers lose the heart and soul of what they should be focusing on in their classrooms. Moreover, there is a large body of literacy research that demonstrates the connection between reading achievement

Recommended Research About Real-World Reading, Motivation, and Achievement

Anderson, R. C., Wilson, P. T., & Fielding, L. G. (1988). Growth in reading and how children spend their time outside of school. *Reading Research Quarterly, 23*(3), 285–303.

Gottfried, A. E. (1990). Academic intrinsic motivation in young elementary school children.

(Continued)

(Continued)

Journal of Educational Psychology, 82(3), 525–538.

Guthrie, J. T. (2007). Reading motivation and reading comprehension growth in the later elementary years. *Contemporary Educational Psychology* 32(3), 282–313.

and reading in real-world contexts. Chapter 5 gives an overview of the research on methods for developing lifelong independent readers by rooting your units in real-world contexts. It includes a section on monitoring at-home reading, the use of book clubs as a scaffolding tool for building independent readers, and the unique reading choices of boys.

CONNECT YOUR READING UNITS TO REAL-WORLD CONTEXTS

By *real-world texts*, I mean texts that students will encounter as adults in their everyday lives. These texts are cross-curricular, nonfiction, fiction, electronic, and print. As was discussed in Chapter 4, the best motivators are intrinsic. If you have a student who is fixated on a topic (dinosaurs, Star Wars, the Cubs, Brett Favre, Egyptians, skin care), then you have an opportunity to get that student hooked on reading. Graphic novels are a good, transitional medium for readers who are intimidated by a page full of print.

Real-world reading also means learning to read across the curriculum. Guthrie and his team of researchers at the University of Maryland developed a system of Concept-Oriented Reading Instruction (CORI) which is designed to increase the amount of time students spend in engaged reading, which "refers to reading strategically (using background knowledge, questioning, summarizing, and other skills), with the motivational goals of learning from text, interacting with other students to learn, and gaining conceptual understanding of science through reading" (retrieved from the CORI website at http://www.cori.umd.edu/). The system includes monitoring checklists for struggling readers and charts to scaffold summarizing in the science content areas for third and fourth graders.

For those of you in districts with a mandated reading curriculum, don't give up on providing your students with real-world reading opportunities. There are many ways to enhance or supplement the required material. One way that I incorporate this type of opportunity into my reading classes is through reading stations and differentiated instruction groups. While I meet with different groups of students, the rest of the class is working through a menu of stations. It is very easy to add real-world reading to a station. One easy example is one I use during a predetermined reading theme on the American Revolution. For one of the stations, I provide social studies books and other fiction and nonfiction books on the American Revolution. Students are asked to read the books and apply different reading strategies we have worked on. They can also compare and contrast a fiction and nonfiction book on the period. Another example of incorporating real-world reading is within the actual differentiated reading groups. By choosing different types of reading (magazines, newspapers, short stories, novels, cartoons, etc.) to practice our strategies, hopefully students will see the real-world significance of what we are learning in reading class.

TEACHING STUDENTS TO READ FOR PLEASURE

Don't give up on providing time for your students to practice reading for pleasure in school. Whether you call it Drop Everything and Read (DEAR) or Sustained Silent Reading (SSR) or free reading, make sure you make time for students to explore reading materials independently.

In 2000, the National Reading Panel published a report called *Teaching Children to Read* (the thirty-five-page report can be downloaded online at http://www.nationalreadingpanel.org/Publications/summary.htm). The report reviewed published research on the effectiveness of independent silent reading in the classroom. Most of the research that has been conducted on SSR is correlational, suggesting that students who read more are more fluent, but it could also be that students who are better readers just choose to read more (National Reading Panel, 2000, p. 12). The results of the meta-analysis were mixed; in the end, the panel was not able to recommend SSR as a practice to improve reading achievement because of the lack of scientifically based studies that may or may not support what intuitively seems like a good idea.

For SSR to be effective, the teachers have to provide modeling for what is supposed to happen during independent reading. Children need access to good books that are interesting, and teachers need to model reading along with the children. One of the ways I model what good readers do when they read is to read chapter books out loud to the class. It prepares students to independently use the same strategies when they read by themselves.

Chapter Books I Like to Read Aloud to My Class

Mrs. Frisby and the Rats of Nimh by Robert C. O'Brien

The Enormous Egg by Oliver Butterworth

Superfudge by Judy Blume

The Watsons Go to Birmingham 1963 by Christopher Paul Curtis

The Witches by Roald Dahl

Charlotte's Web by E. B. White

Ideas to Use When You Read a Chapter Book Out Loud to Your Class

- Write letters to the characters in the story.
- Develop an illustrated dictionary for the class using the vocabulary in the book.
- Make a prediction chart on poster board set up by date (see Figure 5.1).

Figure 5.1

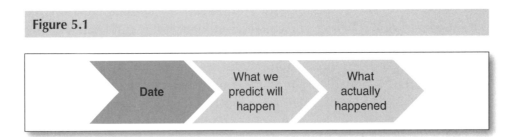

- Before you read for the day, have students meet in groups of three or four to make a list of questions from the previous day's reading, for which they would like answers.

The Value of SSR for Struggling Readers

Researcher Richard Allington gave a talk to K–12 literacy instructors at our local school district where he pointed out that lower achieving students are usually pulled out of silent reading to read aloud to a teacher, either in a small group with other struggling readers or alone. Either way, as he points out in his book, *What Really Matters for Struggling Readers,* children who read alone would read 400 words for every 100 words the oral reading children would read (Allington, 2006, p. 37). Since we know that the key to becoming proficient at reading is practice, the differences in the amount of reading that students read should be a point of concern for teachers. So if we decide that struggling readers need to read at least as much if not more than proficient readers, we need to provide them with opportunities to read materials that sustain their interest. (Chapter 4 explored specific ways to motivate and engage students.)

A word about the phrase *free reading*—free reading is never really "free." I used to tell my eighth graders that I was open to them reading just about anything during SSR; so long as they understood that I reserved the right to talk to their parents about their choices. For example, a John Deere tractor catalog is fine, but *Playboy* is not. One year, I interrupted a group of sixth graders giggling in the corner around an issue of *Seventeen* magazine. When I asked to see the article, the girls turned bright red as I was handed a chart titled, "What your boyfriend's underwear says about him."

I confiscated the magazine and showed it to the girl's mom. That was the end of her *Seventeen* magazine subscription.

For my personal reading pleasure, I read the news online, I'll browse *People* magazine, I will flip through the *New Yorker* looking at cartoons and fiction by people I've heard of, and at night I might read a novel recommended to me by a friend, usually something with a turquoise or peach cover clearly marketed toward middle-aged women. How will your students grow up to be adults who read for pleasure if they don't figure out what they like when they are young?

Preparing Students for Free Reading

When I introduce free reading to my fifth graders, I start off by asking them what type of reading they see parents doing at home. We make a list of the reading in their homes. The list usually includes newspapers, magazines, books, manuals for new appliances, instructions for putting together a new piece of furniture, and forms and letters from school. This leads us to discuss why I don't require them to read a certain number of chapter books each grading period and to take tests on them. That is just not what adults do! My students are so excited to read whatever they want. At the beginning of the year, I have tons of magazines and video game manuals in my classroom, but as the novelty wears off, the kids generally, naturally, find their way to books for most of their reading. One of the favorites year after year is a hunting safety manual. Living in a very rural state, this is a big deal for most fifth graders: passing hunter's safety. They love that they can read their manual in class without having to sneak it in, and my kids always pass! I like to attribute it to the fact that they have actually had time to read the manual, unlike other kids.

The important thing to remember is that reading in real-world contexts should not be ruined by the teacher's insisting that the student produce something after he or she finishes reading. I heard Lucy Calkins put it this way: when I am lying in bed and I finish a book, I don't close it, turn to my husband and say, "Wow. That was a great book. Honey, will you pass me the glue so I can start a diorama?"

All of this means that silent reading time in your classroom needs to be less controlled. Don't pull kids aside and make them read out loud to you from a book they are reading for pleasure and then ask them to summarize what they've read. More importantly, don't limit what kids can choose to read for pleasure based on some external rating system of reading ability or grade level.

One last note on getting kids to read: it is important for kids to know what *you* are reading. Maybe it is unrealistic to expect to find time to read for pleasure in your classroom when your students may need your help during SSR. But that doesn't mean you shouldn't be discussing what you are reading, whether it is a children's book or not. Find ways to bring up what you are reading. Maybe something in math reminds you of the chapter you read last night in your mystery book. When kids see you relating your reading to everyday experiences, it becomes very powerful for them.

At the beginning of this school year, I noticed a student new to our school reading a kid's book I had picked up during the summer. We started talking about the book and where we were in it. This went on for a couple days, and this student, a very competitive fifth-grade boy, challenged me to see who could finish reading the book first. He ended up winning and earned the class an extra recess for beating the teacher at reading a book. By the end of the third week of school, this new student had made connections with me as a reader as well as with other students in the class who read the same book. Your students need to know that you too read for enjoyment outside of school.

READING AT HOME: W.E.I.R.D.

I was very fortunate to have Mrs. Brigid Gerace as my mentor teacher in Chicago Public Schools in 1992, when I was doing my training to become an elementary school teacher. She created an at-home reading program for our third graders called W.E.I.R.D. (We Enjoy Independent Reading Daily). Each week, the students were expected to complete at least 15 minutes of reading at home. It didn't matter if they read the newspaper, a magazine, a cookbook, a comic book, or a novel.

We created W.E.I.R.D. folders for each student by stapling a sheet (see Figure 5.2) into a manila folder. The students would log what they read and how much time they read in the folder. Students were required to read a total of 15 hours per semester, and we kept a chart on the wall where we tracked each student's independent reading progress in 5-hour increments.

The purpose of the W.E.I.R.D reading program was to provide students with an opportunity to practice reading for pleasure at home. The reading selections are student driven and student paced, just as in the real world.

Figure 5.2 W.E.I.R.D. Folder Insert to Staple Inside a Manila Folder

We Enjoy Independent Reading Daily

W.E.I.R.D. Folder

What You Read	Date	Number of Minutes You Read	Parent Signature
Charlotte's Web	9/3/2012	20 min	J.LaGrone
Charlotte's Web	9/4/2012	15 min	J.LaGrone
Charlotte's Web	9/5/2012	15 min	J.LaGrone
Horton Hears a Who	9/7/2012	30 min	J.LaGrone
Total for Week: 1 hour 20 minutes			

SOURCE: From a concept used by Mrs. Brigid Gerace, my preservice teaching mentor who retired from Chicago Public Schools after thirty-four years.

I have implemented the W.E.I.R.D. reading program into my classroom. Not only are my kids thrilled to get to read anything they want, but I have turned W.E.I.R.D. into a competition between my morning and afternoon reading groups. They love it. Not only are the class minutes posted on the board throughout the week, the winning class gets "bragging rights" until the next week. No candy or pizza parties and I truly feel my students are developing a love for reading.

WHAT'S THE DEAL WITH BOYS?

So on the last day of school, I was sitting in my car at the bus stop, waiting for the kids. I was reading *The Lightning Thief* by Rick Riordan. It's a young-adult novel based on Greek mythology with the premise that kids with Attention-Deficit/Hyperactivity Disorder (ADHD) are half-breeds with a Greek god as a parent. My friend at work had given me her copy, and I couldn't put it down. As the kids got dropped off, I could hear them, but I didn't want to put my book down. As the fourth-grade neighbor boy walked by, he stopped and stared at me. His mom walked over to see why Avery was looking at me. I looked up from the book as his mom said, "Oh, Avery reads those books." I looked at Avery.

"Wait. Books . . . you mean there's more than one?"

Now Avery, this kid who probably has only spoken maybe ten words to me in his whole life, lights up and says, "Oh, yeah. There are *four*. I'm number twenty-two on the waitlist at the library for the fourth one. It just came out."

So that day, I finished binge reading the book. Then I went to the library and got books two and three. I looked at the waitlist and saw that I would be number fifty-two for the fourth book. Forget it. I bought the fourth book at the mall. I then proceeded to read all of the books in the series by the end of the weekend. When I was done, I walked down to the neighbor's house. Avery's dad answered the door.

"Um . . . Is Avery home?" I held up the book as if that were an explanation.

Avery came around the corner, I handed him the book, and he looked right at me with big eyes as if I had just handed him a winning lottery ticket. "I just finished it. It was awesome. When you're done you totally need to call me so we can talk about it. I can't believe we have to wait another year for him to write the fifth book!"

Later that afternoon I was in the garden weeding and Avery's dad stopped by as he was walking his dog. He said, "Avery hasn't stopped reading that book since you came by. He's on page 220."

"I *know*! Those books are awesome. I don't know how anyone can put them down." The dad looked at me as if I was crazy.

Look—when you find a book that you like, you give it to someone. Now I just happen to be the kind of person who likes fantasy books— monsters, fairies, elves, goblins, witches, dementors, Greek gods, what- ever. And so that means that I fall into the same target demographic as a middle-school boy. I'm convinced that's what makes me a good teacher of kids that age; I don't fake my enthusiasm for fantasy books. So when I wait in line for the newest *Lord of the Rings* or *Harry Potter* movie, I invariably find myself in line with some of my students—and *all* of us read the books first.

The point is this: we read what we like. And most elementary school teachers are women who like stories about strong young girls who over- come some odds (think: *Out of the Dust*, or *Catherine Called Birdy*, or *Little Women*, or *Matilda*—you get the point). So what is a young boy supposed to think when those are all the books that keep getting assigned at school?

Reading is *lame* for boys (and girls like me) who don't like the books the teachers are picking for the whole class to read.

According to the Eco-Libris website (n.d.), 55 percent of fiction is bought by women, 45 percent by men. If you are more interested in the uniqueness of boys and their reading choices, I highly recommend visiting the British national literacy trust website to view their research on boys and literacy: http://www.literacytrust.org.uk/database/boys/English .html. So what's the answer? Choices.

LITERATURE CIRCLES AND BOOK CLUBS: WHAT IS NORMAL IN THE REAL WORLD?

The best thing you can do is come up with a text set around a theme. I used genres. Select enough titles so that you will have about four or five kids in a group reading the same book. Then let the kids choose.

The hardest thing to do as a teacher is to release a little bit of control and let the kids choose their own books so they can start figuring out, on their own, what they like. Make a multilevel survival text set and let the kids choose which of those books they want to read. The American Library Association posts suggestions for books for every age group and interest category. These are books I would recommend with upper elementary school kids with reading levels ranging from fifth grade to eighth grade:

- Laurie Halse Anderson's *Fever, 1793*
- Paul Zindel's *Raptor*
- *Downriver* by Will Hobbs
- Jules Verne's *A Journey to the Centre of the Earth*
- *The Escape From Home* by Avi
- *Hatchet* by Gary Paulsen

Providing books with multiple reading levels also allows you to individualize your instruction, since not everyone has the same interests and abilities. The leveling that is provided by publishing companies can be used as a rough guide, but realize that some of the scales may be off by as much as a grade level one way or the other. It's better to gently steer struggling readers to easier books they will like and have success with than to just announce that some of the books in the text set are *too hard* for certain students.

I especially like books that have sequels, so that kids can read the next book(s) for fun when they are finished.

Here's how your kids will choose their book groups at first:

- Who else is reading that book?
  - Is that person cool?
  - Do I want to be in a group with that person?
  - What is my best friend doing?

This is normal. How many books have you read because a friend handed it to you and said, "You will love this book. I just read it. It is fantastic."

- What does the cover look like?
  - Does it look like a boy book or a girl book?

This is normal. It's what grownups do. My friend chooses books at Barnes and Noble by browsing anything that looks pink or turquoise. She says it's the best way to guarantee that it's a good poolside easy read.

- Is there a movie based on this book?
  - Did I see the movie?
  - Do I want to see the movie?
  - Did the trailers look good?

This is normal. This is also why J. K. Rowling is credited with turning so many nonreaders on to reading. Kids saw the *Harry Potter* movies and wanted to read the books.

The goal is to have a classroom full of kids who have all had the experience of a book they couldn't put down. You can't possibly know what that is going to be for each kid. Don't even try. Children's book publishing is a multibillion dollar a year industry.

According to the trends tracked by the Association of American Publishers (www.publishers.org/main/IndustryStats/indStats_02.htm), in 2007 hardbound sales of titles for children and young adults (juvenile) fell slightly by 0.5 percent to $2.0 billion compared to 2006, but paperbound increased 4.1 percent to $1.4 billion. Over the longer term, the trend from 2002 to 2007 indicates juvenile books are performing well, with compound annual growth rates of 4.6 percent for hardbound and 2.1 percent for paperbound. Estimates do not include the *Harry Potter* series.

The point is that there is a book out there for everyone. Trust me.

BEST PRACTICE FOR BOOK CLUBS

There are decades of research into the best ways to model reading comprehension strategies in small groups with students of all ages. I found success with Harvey Daniels's *Literature Circles* (2001) when I taught elementary school, and Nancie Atwell's *In the Middle* (1998) when I worked with middle schoolers. My intent is not to advocate for one or the other, but to point out that there are multiple approaches to providing students with formalized settings for talking about books. Both Daniels and Atwell advocate providing a wide range of choices for readers as a way to prepare children for reading in real-world contexts. Older students are able to make decisions about a reading schedule and the role for book club, while younger students will need a teacher to make those decisions for them. Also, children who have had several years of experience participating in book clubs will need less guidance than children who are experiencing it for the first time in your classroom. The teacher's role in the book club is to guide the reading with intentional questioning and to model for students how to interrogate the texts (for instance, Why is there an alligator on the cover of the book? Why did the author spend so much time describing the mother's favorite hat? Do you think the alligator is going to do something to the hat? Why is that character helping the alligator write a letter to the mother?).

More important, teachers need to form their own professional book clubs, not just for the adult companionship, but also for the professional development opportunities book clubs can present, especially in a district that might not be able to afford to bring in high-powered speakers or purchase expensive, instructional programs. I have spoken with groups of teachers who have found success creating building-wide adult book clubs using professional development texts like Harvey and Goudvis's *Strategies That Work: Teaching Comprehension to Enhance Understanding* (2000). The purpose of the book club can be twofold: a chance for professional development with colleagues, and an opportunity to problem-solve and experiment with expert readers (teachers), using innovative, teacher-developed, literature-circle strategies. Of course an added bonus is that it gives teachers something to read in SSR as they are modeling for their own students the many different purposes adults have for reading.

Building or school principals looking for good books to use for staff development can find a myriad of resources online. Start with the library on the Literacy Coaching Clearinghouse website (www.literacycoaching online.org/library.html), compiled by the National Council of Teachers of English and the International Reading Association.

SUMMARY

Connecting student reading to real-world contexts *is* best practice in literacy education. This means making sure that your students have multiple opportunities to read for pleasure, and it means giving readers an opportunity to make choices about what they will read. Remember: practice makes perfect. Give your students lots of chances to practice reading silently to themselves for their own purposes. Don't limit the choices based on unscientific and undependable reading scales that yield unreliable grade level designations.

At the same time, don't dismiss the realities of test preparation. Approach the tests themselves as a genre to be studied: a code to be cracked.

END-OF-CHAPTER QUIZ

Mr. Streeter's fourth-grade class this year has a very cliquey group of girls, which includes seven of the twelve girls in the class. When he announces that there are four books in the series for book clubs in the next unit, the seven girls instantly begin talking to each other about being in a group together. Mr. Streeter hasn't even announced the books or the theme for the unit yet!

What should he do?

1. Ignore the girls and keep going.

2. Give a book talk for each book, and then make everyone in the class silently write the title of the book they want to read. Form the groups based on preference.

3. Make the groups up so that the five girls not in the clique are evenly spread out among the other girls.

4. Make a rule about the number of boys and girls who need to be in each book club.

5. Acknowledge that people choose to read books based on lots of factors, including friends in book clubs, but remind the girls not to behave in a way that might exclude others in the class.

6. Tell the girls they can only be with each other for group work once per semester, and make them decide if this is going to be one of those times.

6 Best Practice

Chapter Highlights

- Raising test scores
- Making inservices count
- Theoretical approaches to elementary reading

Don't compromise what you know to be *best practice* in teaching reading. So many of us feel the pressure from the high-stakes accountability system that we desperately search for any quick curriculum fix, especially if our school is not making adequate yearly progress (AYP) under the No Child Left Behind Act (NCLB).

Chapter 6 describes some of the work that is being done in the field to raise test scores, reviews the outlets for finding out about research on the efficacy of those teaching practices, and describes quality inservices. In addition, the chapter reviews the research on several theoretical approaches to teaching reading in the elementary school—reader response theory, critical literacy, and the use of multicultural literature—so that teachers can determine which blend of approaches will work in their given instructional context.

I was conducting field research in one school that switched to a test-preparation curriculum consisting of two hours' worth of worksheets in the weeks leading up to the state test. These worksheets were mock versions of the kinds of test items that would appear on the test for reading and vocabulary. As soon as the test was over, the teachers switched back to their regular curriculum, which was based on Harvey and Goudvis's *Strategies That Work* (Harvey & Goudvis, 2000). For both the students and the teachers, the worksheets were like a nasty, bad-tasting medicine. When I asked the teachers why they were using the worksheets, they said it was because they were afraid that if their school didn't make AYP for a second year, they would be reorganized by the state.

This absolutely baffles me.

If what you've been doing during the year is what you know to be the best way to teach, how are skill-and-drill worksheets going to help, right before the test? Especially when you know that you have conducted an alignment study and you are confident that you are teaching the kids the literacy skills that the test is supposed to measure.

Have confidence in yourself as a professional. Best practice is *best practice* year round.

Teachers must hold their ground. If your school is under pressure to raise test scores, it is important to evaluate your teaching and curriculum to be sure it is the best it can be. Ask the people making decisions about curriculum in your district for evidence of effectiveness and demand that the programs are reevaluated every year.

There's a great book called *Test Driven* by Valli, Croninger, Chambliss, Graeber, and Buese (2008) that I read with my graduate students in a doctoral seminar at the University of Iowa. The researchers describe the way three schools are dealing with the pressures of the accountability movement in their classrooms. One of our more lively class discussions came from the use of a "triage model" by one of the schools, where teachers focus on test-preparation lessons for students who are on the proficiency bubble. In other words, students who are just on the edge of being counted as proficient on the state NCLB test receive special instruction designed to artificially raise their test scores. The teachers interviewed in *Test Driven* describe the tension between teaching and test preparation, particularly the pressure to teach all of the district standards and still prepare the students for the test. Sometimes the impetus for these kinds of targeted instruction for "bubble students" comes from the school administrators putting teachers in the position of trying to reconcile how test preparation and reading instruction can be two different things.

If you find yourself working under an oppressive administration that believes teachers are a group to be managed and that scripted curriculum is the answer to raising test scores, do not forget about the power of the school board to fight administrative pressure to make curricular changes. Administrators are encouraged to be instructional leaders, but sometimes their educational backgrounds are not in reading. In those instances, you will find them welcome partners in implementing best practices across the school.

Arm yourself with research about the literacy programs you use in your classroom. A good place for you to check for research that has been conducted on the efficacy of various literacy programs is the What Works Clearinghouse (WWC at http://ies.ed.gov/ncee/wwc/). This is a site managed by the U.S. Department of Education that synthesizes scientifically based educational research that has been conducted using various methodologies and gives teachers the bottom line on whether or not a curriculum or program really shows success. For the most part, the articles that are referenced in WWC are founded in experimental and quasi-experimental research.

You may be surprised to see that many of the most popular, commercial reading programs have been found to be utterly ineffective as programs to teach children to read. As Allington points out in his book, *What Really Matters for Struggling Readers* (2006) , the teacher guides to your text books are filled with worksheets, graphic organizers, crossword puzzles, questions for students to answer, word searches, and vocabulary definition tasks: tasks that, as Allington puts it, "simply assessed whether or not students could adequately respond" (p. 121).

WHAT DO QUALITY INSERVICES LOOK LIKE?

A fifth-grade teacher called to tell me about a three-day workshop her school district had mandated for all K–6 language arts teachers. The presenter spent the first two days of the workshop modeling for the teachers how to have children sound out words. After six hours of this inservice, the teachers were openly reading magazines, looking through catalogs, filing their nails, talking to one another, and planning lessons for the first week of school; it was a complete and utter waste of time because the workshop did not address anything substantive that could be done in the classroom to prepare teachers with strategies for struggling readers. At one point, the presenter asked if anyone knew what *orthography* means. My friend said she shouted out "spelling" without looking up, and the workshop facilitator spent the rest of the day calling her the *gifted* student.

Seriously!

Any reading workshop that begins with the premise that you are stupid, or lazy, or too stubborn to be taught a new way to teach, or worse yet uneducated, is unproductive. At the same time, being rude (like openly filing your nails and flipping through a magazine) does nothing to enhance the reputation of public school teachers as a group of professionals.

It is time for us to take back our professional development. We have all been through preservice teacher training already. We have strategies in our toolbox for teaching people how to read. However, when there is exciting new research or an approach to teaching reading, all of us should be open to it. But we do not need to tolerate being talked down to in an inservice. I don't know if it's because teaching is a female-dominated profession but I can't think of any other field where workers are too polite to speak up when a professional development experience isn't worth their time. But filing your nails or grading papers isn't an appropriate alternative. Maybe we need a new definition for "professional development"—a definition that is more along the lines of "coaching."

In their book, Bean and Morewood (2007) describe some of the best practices in professional development: literacy coaching, building communities of learners, teacher research, and online courses are listed as popular ways reading teachers improve their practice. Whatever the strategy, we know that school leadership is a key ingredient to the successful implementation of any new curricular approach (p. 390). You absolutely need to have your principal on board with what you are doing in your classrooms to ensure that your professional development activities are aligned with your practice. To do this, you need to be able to articulate the way you approach the teaching of reading.

THEORY AND PRACTICE AT THE ELEMENTARY LEVEL: BEST PRACTICES PRIMER

Think about how you teach literature in your classroom. See if you can figure out which academic theory is guiding your instruction. For most teachers, we find ourselves using a blend of different theories in our practice. Some of these approaches are grounded in research that is reviewed in the WWC, and some of it is purely theoretical. I provide several academic sources in this section, in case you would like to read more about these theoretical frameworks for approaching the teaching of reading. As you read, ask yourself which approach sounds most like what you do.

Reader Response Theory in the Elementary School

In the elementary school, the predominant approach to teaching reading is neither text based nor author based but, rather, a reader-centered approach where elementary teachers ask children to relate their own life experiences to the stories they read in class. The way this approach has been practiced in schools "is to highlight the life of the reader through personal response" (Lewis, 2000).

The term that is used to describe this way of talking about books is often called *reader response,* especially as articulated by Rosenblatt in her 1995 text *Literature as Exploration.* In the literary transaction between the individual reader's response and the text, the reader's job is to make connections to the text and to see the ways the characters and other elements of the story relate to the reader's own life. Rosenblatt explains that "the same text will have a very different meaning and value to us at different times or under different circumstances" (p. 35). Rosenblatt views reading as a transaction, "a two-way process, involving a reader and a text at a particular time under particular circumstances" (Rosenblatt, 1982, p. 268). This is not a transaction that necessarily involves the author, but rather it privileges the reader above all else.

The Reader-Centered Approach

In a reader response classroom, the role of the reader is crucial in determining the meaning of a text (Nodelman, 2003), and the focus is on student responses based on their experiences with similar texts, their emotions, or their own member resources (i.e., their race, gender, or class).

One of the problems with the reader-centered approach is the limitations of prior knowledge when the young reader hasn't had the life experience one would need in order to make a personal connection to the text (Lewis, 2000). What happens when children are asked to make personal connections to a text that describes an experience that is very different from their own? Marshall (2000) concludes his summary of new research in the field of response to literature with a question about the pedagogical implications if a reader response classroom is using multicultural texts to make sense of the world. He writes that "teachers and students, in such a context, cannot rely on a process of identification with characters or situations (these characters are like me and therefore I can identify with them" (p. 397).

For example, the picture book *Fly Away Home* (Bunting, 1991), about a homeless father and son who are living in an airport, is not a story to which most suburban, middle-class children can concretely relate. Yes, perhaps they have been to an airport. But that isn't the point of the story. What can privileged children bring to a text about homelessness, in the reader response classroom, that will help them understand homelessness in a way that makes them want to become socially active? Some elementary teachers are finding that reader response theory isn't always appropriate as an instructional tool and have begun to try to incorporate components of critical literacy into the literature curriculum. This isn't wholly out of alignment with reader response. As Hynds and Appleman (1997) observe, Rosenblatt's (1995) second stated purpose in *Literature as Exploration* was to "highlight the social and political role of literature in a democracy" (p. 274), and this aim has been largely ignored until recently.

Critical Literacy

Since the late 1990s, as critical theory began to manifest itself in American elementary schools, practice shifted to a focus on literature as a nonneutral cultural practice (Luke & Freebody, 1997; Vasquez, 2003) and has been described as the critical literacy approach. Like Luke and Freebody (1997), I use the term critical literacy to refer to a pedagogy that "encourages the development of alternative reading positions and practices for questioning and critiquing texts and their affiliated social formations and cultural assumptions" (p. 218). The elementary teacher's role in these classrooms is to lead discussions about voices that might be silenced in a text or an analysis of discourses that preserve some sociocultural practices and not others. Morgan (1997) writes that

> struggles to define the world and claim its goods are carried out by unequally matched contestants, for certain social groups have historically controlled the ideologies, institutions and practices of their society, thereby maintaining their dominant position. But since these are socially and historically constructed, they can be reconstructed. (p. 1)

Many teachers who embrace this approach do so with an eye to a larger pedagogy with a visible political and social agenda. Comber (2001) explains what happens in a critical literacy classroom:

> when teachers and students are engaged in critical literacy, they will be asking complicated questions about language and power, about people and lifestyle, about morality and ethics, about who is advantaged by the ways things are and who is disadvantaged. (p. 271)

This theory offers elementary teachers the possibilities to teach a whole new set of skills in the classroom, skills often aligned with larger and more overtly political pedagogical goals in the teaching for social justice.

In my room this year we have been reading the book *Crash* by Jerry Spinelli. Our school has been mandated to implement a new bullying program that is very dry and scripted. To supplement this, I chose to read this book aloud. It shows great examples of a kid who is bullied, a kid who bullies, kids who choose to stand by and do nothing, and those few brave enough to stand up for what is right. As we have been reading the book, we have shared such rich dialoguing about why bullying happens, who bullies, why some students seem to be easier targets, and why bystanders don't stand up to these bullies. While critics may think this approach is developmentally inappropriate for elementary students, with guidance and in the confines of a secure classroom environment, I feel confident my students have gained an insight into bullying they wouldn't have attained through the mandated program alone.

Teaching Students to Question What They Read

The trend in many elementary schools now is to examine texts, especially multicultural ones, which present readers with the opportunity to critique the ideologies of the author and the text, as well as their own. Corcoran (1994) writes that a teacher in a critical literacy-based classroom "wants students to develop an ability to challenge a text's ideology when appropriate, to see that texts arrive with socially constructed values, even biases and prejudices, some of which may not be supportive of the reader's best interests (p. x)."

In the K–8 critical literacy classroom, teachers are asking readers to question the way participants (the readers, the characters, the authors) are socially constructed, a sort of mixing of text- and reader-centered strategies (Hynds & Appleman, 1997; Lewis, 2000). It is a postmodern pedagogy that still gives students the freedom to make connections between their lives and the texts they encounter in school, but the difference is that the instructor is asking students to question those connections in terms of power relations and ideologies (e.g., *Why does it surprise you as a reader when it is revealed that Jesse is actually a girl? How have her behaviors up to this point been constructed as "male"?*). Using this blend of critical literacy and reader response, individual responses to literature are informed by the individual's own sociopolitical context (Beach, 1993, Corcoran, 1992). The teacher's new role is to create critical readers as opposed to simply responsive readers.

Critical literacy skills are practiced using books for children where the authors' and readers' visible ideologies can stimulate critical conversations in classrooms. Students are asked to become aware of how systems of meaning and power affect people's lives in an effort to promote social justice (Harste, 2000; Lewison, Seely Flint, & Van Sluys, 2002; McGillis, 1997; Soter, 1999; Yenika-Agbaw, 1997). Luke, O'Brien, and Comber (2001) argue that "critical literacy sets out to encourage students to begin to see that literate practice is always morally and politically loaded—and that to work with a text doesn't necessarily involve uncritically buying into its world view or position" (p. 122).

Critical Literacy in the Elementary School

Critics of critical literacy question whether this approach is developmentally appropriate at the elementary level. But primary teachers like Luke (1994), Martínez-Roldán and López-Robertson (2000) and Vasquez (2003) describe their experiences using critical literacy with very young primary students, talking thoughtfully about literature and exploring the ways certain texts may or may not exclude certain groups.

For example, Vasquez's Australian junior kindergartners searched the school library for books about Malta and Peru, because two students in the class had emigrated from there. The absence of these books prompted a discussion about dominant ethnicities and equitable representation in the contents of the school library. As part of a social action approach to literacy, Vasquez helped the children write letters to the school librarian suggesting the purchase of books that represented the ethnicities of all of the children in their class. Vasquez concludes that this is an approach to the curriculum that is suitable for all ages and that even very small children can begin to question the way things are in our world. She describes a primary school curriculum rooted in the theory of critical literacies and built on the cultural questions children have about everyday life (Vasquez, 2001).

Critical literacy asks teachers to facilitate the reconstruction of dominant ideologies by teaching that texts are open to a variety of readings given the different histories, backgrounds, and experiences of the authors and the readers (Leland & Harste, 2000). The ability to read texts (defined broadly) in different ways is a skill that is at the heart of the larger goals of this pedagogy: to help students develop a "disposition for principled evaluation of cultural products" (Morgan, 1997). In this way, "texts are regarded as constructs which promote interested versions of reality" (O'Neill, 1993). The text is understood to be culturally constructed, so the reader is not solely responsible for finding meaning. Thus critical literacy is a reader-oriented approach to literary theory that asks the reader to develop reading practices that respect the cultural politics of various groups (Corcoran, 1994).

Multicultural Literature
in the Service of Teaching Critical Literacy

To promote cultural understanding, many teachers are turning to multicultural literature as a teaching tool to redefine diversity (Creighton, 1997; Enciso, 1997; Fang, Fu, & Lamme, 1999). Comber (1999) writes that the protagonists of critical literacy come from "feminist standpoints, critical linguists, poststructuralist theory, antiracism, the work of Paolo Freire, and more" (p. 2). In keeping with the political commitment and educational agendas of these protagonists, the kind of literature that has been used in the elementary classroom to serve the needs of the critical literacy teacher has typically been multicultural literature featuring books that "honor diversity and invite students and teachers alike to explore a new kind of literacy curriculum—one built upon the premise that a model of difference is a model of learning for individuals in society" (Luke & Freebody, 1997).

The purpose of including multicultural literature in the curriculum, according to Nieto (1992), is to "challenge and reject racism and other forms of discrimination in schools and society and accept and affirm the pluralism (ethnic, racial, linguistic, religious, economic, and gender, among others) that students, their communities, and teachers represent" (p. 208). This has resonated with teachers, and in fact the market for multicultural books written for children has grown exponentially since teachers began using it in their classrooms; the Coretta Scott King Award for multicultural literature now has a sales impact comparable to the Newbery and Caldecott Medals.

Using Multicultural Literature With Elementary Classes

One of the criticisms of the use of multicultural literature in the elementary school is the underlying assumption of this pedagogy that books have the power to change people's ideologies. Is it unrealistic to expect that literature has the power to change lives and erase intolerant behaviors in the world? Harris (1994) cautions against burdening children's books with the responsibility of reforming society (p. 12). How contested is the presumption that children become what they read? Surely for generations fairy tales have been used as cautionary tales to frighten children into behaving a certain way (e.g., Hansel and Gretel—don't talk to strangers; they might be witches in disguise who will cook you in an oven and eat you!). Marshall (2000) uses the more contemporary example of William Bennett's *The Book of Virtues*, as an example of this ideology at work. Maybe it's not just multicultural books in isolation that can redress intolerant ideologies, but perhaps the books lend themselves to a different kind of classroom discourse that can provide a forum for talking about social justice that *can* have long-lasting effects.

Multicultural remains a contested term (Cai, 1998; Harris, 1996), and debates among scholars rage about whether the race of the author should matter, whether an "outsider" to a culture can accurately portray it, and what texts can qualify as multicultural (Banks, 1996; Barrera, Liguori, & Salas, 1993; Cai & Bishop, 1994; Lasky, 1996; Wolf, Ballentine, & Hill, 1999). Another criticism of the way multiculturalism is executed in the classrooms comes from researchers like Hade (1997), who writes that multiculturalism is about challenging mainstream discourse and should not be reduced to a tourism approach where readers travel to other cultures but are "no less ignorant in how to effect real change" (p. 240).

Political Tensions to Consider
When Choosing Multicultural Literature

There is tension when the pedagogical goals of a progressive, multicultural education are not necessarily aligned with the reasons that teachers might be using multicultural literature in their classrooms. Taxel (1997) historically situates the political debate about multicultural children's books in schools in terms of the rise of conservative Republicans to political power and the backlash since the turn of the century against multicultural literature and political correctness. He defends multicultural literature as reflective of "the rich cultural mosaic that is our nation, as well as the very highest literary and artistic standards" (p. 444).

Another point of contention in the literature about the use of the term multicultural to modify literature is that it could be construed as just a code for "brown." These scholars argue that all texts are multicultural and that the mere classification of literature into a category of multicultural, ironically only serves to further normalize "whiteness." For example, Wollman-Bonilla (1998) writes that "educators designate books 'multicultural' if they represent other cultures, whereas books reflecting a Eurocentric perspective are viewed as normative" (pp. 287–88). But despite this bickering in the ivory tower (Cai, 1998), the less-complicated goal for many elementary teachers in the classroom is to find well-written books for children that deal with issues of diversity in developmentally appropriate and culturally sensitive ways. Because the reader response approach traditionally has not been interested in the author, most elementary teachers have not embraced the debate about author and authenticity.

Talking About Race With Elementary Students

Some teachers are using this multicultural literature in the service of a new kind of curriculum that allows for conversations about race and ideology. Edelsky (1999) argues that

> a critical pro-justice curriculum has to provide the kind of safety that lets teachers and students figure out how to have the tough, honest conversations about race, gender, and class that put all the pain and problems on the table but yet strengthen, rather than weaken, intergroup ties (p. 7).

She explains that a "critical pedagogy works at figuring out where the taken-for-granted, business-as-usual came from, what it's connected to, and whose interests it serves." (p. 15) Elementary teachers are accepting this approach to literature and are asking different questions in the classroom.

Educators argue that multicultural literature isn't the only kind of text that is appropriate for a critical analysis. In a multicultural context, a seemingly mundane text can reveal as much about culture, society, power, and identity as a more complex text. However, other researchers suggest that multicultural literature specifically provides a unique forum for conversations about race, gender, and culture.

KNOW WHAT WORKS FOR YOU

There is no one right way to teach reading, despite what the paid facilitator of your latest inservice wants you to think. Of course these things are contextual: the age level of your students, the racial and ethnic mix in your community, and your comfort level with these theoretical frameworks should guide what you do from year to year. The bottom line here is this: don't give in to the fads presented at the inservices, and fight for your right to have professional development activities that will support your practice. Your time is too valuable to be wasted!

END-OF-CHAPTER QUIZ

The vice principal has noticed that the lowest score on the state test for the school last year was vocabulary. To remedy this, she decides to institute a new "word of the week" for the entire school. Over the intercom each Monday, VP announces the word: "Good morning boys and girls. This week's word of the week is 'drought'." The teachers in each classroom write the word on the board, ask the students to look up the meaning in a dictionary, and encourage the children to use the word throughout the week.
    Discuss the ethicality of the word of the week.

1. What if the VP uses the vocabulary words from old forms of the state test? Current forms?

2. What if the words were generated by the teachers?

3. What if an incentive system were put into place? For example, kids could earn a star on a chart every time they used the word of the week in class correctly in context. A test could be made each month with the four words from that month and administered to the entire student body. Classes with the highest score would earn a pizza party.

4. What do we know about the best ways to teach vocabulary? How does the word-of-the-week system align with what we know about best practice?

7 Implications for Your Teaching and Beyond

Chapter Highlights

- Reviewing what a balanced reading program looks like
- Test misuse from a historical perspective
- How to get your principal on your side

HOLDING YOUR GROUND

A balanced reading instructional program requires an opportunity for students to read independently, to read for pleasure, and to practice behaviors that expert readers exhibit, including talking about books in social contexts (for example, in book clubs). In addition, emerging and struggling readers need to be given tools to become independent readers. This might be in the form of individualized lessons for students whose progress and growth are then charted with formative assessments, as described in Chapter 2, or as assistive technology, as discussed in Chapter 3. In this final chapter, themes about the dangers of high-stakes testing are tempered with a discussion of the value of these test scores for instructional purposes. Included in this chapter is a historical perspective on high-stakes testing in Iowa in the 1930s.

Don't Panic

In Miller's (2002) *English Education* essay "Reflective Teaching in the Panic of High-Stakes Testing," she writes, "In the panic of the new high-stakes testing, many young teachers too often receive the message from administrators and the community that scores are more important than students (p. 167). In many school districts as a means to raise test scores, the stakes placed on standardized, multiple-choice achievement test scores create an academic environment where what is tested can affect what is taught, an idea that runs counter to *best practice* for psychometricians and teachers alike. Test developers are sensitive to the unintended impact high-stakes assessments can have on the curriculum. The time has come to begin an open dialogue between the community of teachers and researchers who are interested in the teaching and learning of literacy at all levels and the community of teachers and researchers who build the achievement tests that are used to assess student academic progress.

Standardized achievement tests are being used in schools in ways that most of us agree are not always right for students: whether it be the impact of high-stakes test scores on students (Horn, 2003; Madaus & Clarke, 2001) or the undesirable effects some testing programs have on the science and arts curricula (Jones et al., 1999) or the way teachers are blamed for factors that are largely out of their control as they are "burnt at the high stakes" (Kohn, 2000). Yet our voices seem to be drowned out by journalists, legislators, and policy makers eager to declare the failure of American public schools (e.g., Gross, 2000). Since the 1981 *A Nation at Risk* report, American reading teachers have been under fire, and the current pressure to raise K–12 reading test scores is only the latest in a long history of attacks.

It is important to talk about what multiple-choice, standardized tests of educational achievement *cannot* do in the domain of reading, as well as what they *can* do to help teachers build a profile of student development and growth. The language arts skills that do not lend themselves easily to large-scale testing (such as speaking) should not get short-shrifted in relationship to the skills that do test well.

I agree with the reading teachers who have said they find it worrisome that testing increasingly seems to be driving the curriculum. These criticisms are not new; in fact over forty years ago in an article about the abuses of standardized **aptitude** and **achievement** tests, Furst (1963) wrote, "A most serious charge is that standardized achievement tests exert too much control over curriculum teaching, and learning" (p. 203).

In addition, standardized tests, especially multiple-choice tests, are criticized for not being particularly well suited to test every aspect of the language arts domain: for instance, how to formulate a coherent idea and express it elegantly in writing, or how to read for knowledge as well as pleasure. Conlan (1986, p. 124) remarks that no multiple choice question can be used to discover how well students can express their own ideas in their own words, how well they can marshal evidence to support their arguments, or how well they can adjust to the need to communicate for a particular purpose and to a particular audience. Nor can multiple-choice questions ever indicate whether what the student writes will be interesting to read.

From the perspective of test developers, most would agree completely that it is a valid and important educational goal to teach students to express themselves elegantly in writing, but there is not an easy, inexpensive way to measure this goal for accountability purposes on a large scale. So standardized tests have limitations for what they can test, and those limitations probably affect language arts more than other core academic subjects.

My dad always says that he who does not know history is destined to repeat it. He also says that the only thing needed for evil to triumph is that good men do nothing, but that's probably neither here nor there. . . . A brief look at the early days of testing in Iowa can shed light on how the problems we see today were foreshadowed in the early days of educational testing. Working in a test development program within a college of education, I am uniquely positioned to see the historical underpinnings of tests that were created to help teachers target instruction—tests that trace back to a model of cooperation and consultation between curriculum experts and testing experts.

TEST MISUSE IN THE EARLY DAYS OF TESTING

One of the first statewide testing programs was developed in Iowa in 1928 for use in the Iowa Academic Meet, modeled after athletic track meets that seemed to be overshadowing academics in high schools. E. F. Lindquist first developed this contest to stimulate "renewed interest on the part of pupils in the fundamental activities which enter into a high school education" (Peterson, 1983, p. 1), and the prize for the top students in those early years was a scholarship to the University of Iowa. This meet, informally known as the *Brain Derby* or the *Cranium Contest*, later became the basis for the Iowa Testing Programs. The idea that the school and the students were tested on academics was novel and lead to the eventual creation of the batteries of large-scale achievement tests that exist today.

By 1932, the Iowa Academic Meet had become immensely popular across Iowa, and it became the first test battery to be administered to students in

Iowa. The assessment program included normative data and comprehensive reports of the results. According to the 1934 announcement about the academic meet, school administrators were happy with the effects the competition was having on high schools across Iowa: "The tests increase pupil interest in school work more than any other single factor," and "the scholar has at last attained a prestige and importance equal to that of the athlete" (Peterson, 1983, p. 6). But Lindquist put a stop to the college scholarship portion of the academic meet after a few years because too much emphasis was placed on the competitive features of the contest. As Lindquist (1970) observed, "This led to an overemphasis on the teaching of informational content, and upon the rote learning of facts, since that is what many teachers felt would be most effective in improving test standing" (p. 8). From the beginning, Lindquist saw the potential danger of standardized tests being used for unintended purposes.

But there is a difference between teaching to the test and teaching what is going to be on the test. As Popham (2005) writes, if a teacher is "teaching to the content represented by the test" then this is good teaching (p. 312). But if a teacher is directing instruction specifically toward the items on the test, this is bad instruction. Thorndike and Hagen (1977/1955) call this "putting the cart before the horse" (p. 535). Despite what many teachers believe, we would be hard-pressed to find anyone in the measurement community who believes that this is an appropriate way for schools to design curriculum. In the Iowa Tests of Basic Skills (ITBS) manual, teachers and counselors are advised against using test scores from a single achievement battery to evaluate the effectiveness of the entire instructional program because "the batteries have not been designed to cover the full range of content standards and benchmarks that make up typical school curriculum" (Hoover et al., 2003, p. 12). No single assessment is comprehensive enough to be able to evaluate a school's entire curriculum. Without question, this is the most troubling impact of the high stakes that have been placed on standardized test scores since No Child Left Behind (NCLB).

THE NEED FOR A SUPPORTIVE PRINCIPAL

As any of us who has ever taught in a building with an excellent principal can attest, administrators who are instructional leaders and curriculum experts can make a huge difference in student achievement. Principals who recognize the expertise of their teachers, who value the innovation of staff, who eagerly experiment with new teaching methods learned at professional development conferences are not as rare as they may seem. Don't be afraid to invite your principal to visit your classroom to see the ways you are creating a thriving, literate environment, especially if as we described in Chapter 4, your principal is experimenting with rewards as a means of motivating students to score higher on the tests.

NO MORE TEACHING TO THE TEST

What can we be doing together to keep standardized tests from driving the curriculum? First, test makers should make sure the tests assess broad skills rather than specific content. When a test measures basic skills, it makes it that much harder for schools to artificially inflate scores by teaching to the test.

Second, teachers and school administrators on assessment advisory committees should choose tests that are in alignment with the curricular content the district has already decided is important. Classroom teachers are the curriculum authorities, and test developers rely on and value their expertise. When there is a significant change in the curriculum, the assessments that are used in the district should be reevaluated. In this way, teachers can be sure that the curriculum is driving the assessments, not the other way around.

Third, the testing industry needs to be sure to invite practicing classroom teachers to contribute to the construction and evaluation of the items that are on the tests in order to be certain that there is a connection between what is actually happening in classrooms and what is on the tests. Because reading instruction always seems to be the focus of legislators and policy makers who are interested in education reform, the need is paramount for test makers and English teachers to communicate specifically and clearly. Without a unified voice from the teaching community, there is a risk that the definitions for reading will come from the tests, not from the teachers.

In addition, the test development community needs to improve its communication with the public about appropriate uses of the test scores. The *Standards for Educational and Psychological Testing* (1999) require that test developers provide **validity** evidence for the tests, which in turn, explicitly enumerates appropriate uses for test scores. Often this evidence is buried in manuals that are read only by school district administrators and counselors. If manuals are filled with testing jargon and are not widely available to teachers, parents, and the media, then the testing industry bears some of the blame for the misconceptions about appropriate use.

Teacher-preparation programs should also improve the ways that teachers are trained in the principles of measurement. This would help not only in the interpretation and evaluation of standardized tests but also in the construction of classroom tests. When classroom teachers understand the usefulness and limitations of the standardized test scores and how they fit with their own classroom assessment data, they are better equipped to use those scores to improve and individualize their instruction.

One of the ways communication between teachers and test authors can be improved is during the development and review of state content standards. These are written by curriculum experts who sometimes forget that teachers are not the only academic users of the documents they create. Every state is required by NCLB to demonstrate the technical adequacy of its assessments with an alignment study. In fact, the validity of test score interpretations in a standards-based accountability system hinges on alignment evidence. The problem with the alignment aspect of technical adequacy is that test developers often find themselves working with alignment documents that have been designed mainly for classroom teacher use to ensure instruction and classroom assessments rather than to reflect the intent of the standards.

These standards are not usually written to be test specifications (see Chapter 1); but for the sake of building an alignment, the test developers are asked to treat them as such. Because standards documents have so many users (classroom teachers, administrators, assessment builders), it seems reasonable to expect that all of these users, after using the documents, would have feedback for the state departments of education. Of course, the development of academic content standards should be under the purview of curriculum experts, not measurement experts, but there is currently no system in place for the users to provide comment about how these standards are functioning as test specifications.

NEXT STEPS

In the 1959 *Iowa Tests of Educational Development* manual, "How to Use the Test Results," Lindquist reminded teachers and administrators to consider standardized test scores in context:

> Considered alone, a test score is just a number, as restricted in meaning as is a word read out of context. The context of the score is made up of many parts—the pupil's educational history, abilities, and personality; his environment; the school curriculum, equipment, and instructional procedures. All these factors, and more, contribute to the interpretation that can be made about a score. The reading of test scores in their proper context requires conscientious effort and some guidance. (Peterson, 1983, p. 125)

Reading teachers and researchers should be able to work together with the testing community to keep those scores in their proper context.

Teachers should be given the appropriate measurement tools to be able to talk to parents and other stakeholders about the information their locally developed writing assessments provide and how it relates to the standardized test scores. This can happen with better communication grounded in a healthy dialogue about issues in testing—a dialogue that does not fall back on test bashing and generalizations. In turn, the testing industry should not be oblivious to teachers during test development. An improved assessment system will result only from improved teacher input and cooperation.

In addition, teachers who find themselves working in schools where the administration is asking for an adoption of a test-preparation curriculum, or worse yet, a teacher-proof curriculum complete with scripts—find your voice! Your job is to teach *reading*, not test taking. And if the tests are truly aligned with what you are teaching, then naturally your test scores will be an indication of that.

FINAL THOUGHTS

NCLB caused a myriad of unintended consequences for literacy educators, especially in schools in danger of not meeting AYP (adequate yearly progress). An overemphasis on teaching the portions of the reading domain that are testable with large-scale assessments, such as spelling and finding facts from a reading passage, narrows the language arts curriculum in ways that go against what teachers know is the best way to teach. For example, in order to target reading instruction at students at varying developmental levels, some schools have adopted reading curricula that limit the choices for children's literature if the books are not on a reading level that has been determined by a publishing company to be academically appropriate. Adult readers don't choose books that way so why should we train our children that books must be challenging to be worth reading? Students don't develop a lifelong love of reading without practicing reading books that interest them.

Educators need to hold their ground as professionals and refuse to compromise their teaching practice in the name of higher test scores. The tests themselves are not the problem; in fact, the test scores can provide teachers with valuable information about student performance on basic language arts skills. The practice of teaching only the skills that can be tested leads to a narrowing of the curriculum and to the deprofessionalization of teachers. It is crucial that administrators, parents, and policy makers realize that the expertise of teachers must be brought to bear on curriculum decisions at the classroom level.

Resource A

Answers to Quizzes

CHAPTER 1

These *Quizzes* are designed to get you and your colleagues talking about best practice. If you want to assign yourself points, then give yourself 5 points if you said *D*, 4 points if you said *E*, 3 points for *B*, 2 points for *C*, and if you said *A*, then you don't get any points at all, because that was the worst answer! It's very possible that capitalization exercises will help fill the holes in Mrs. Brown's lesson plans. Once you have conducted your alignment study and had a team consultation with the other teachers in your area, you should have enough background information to analyze the data from the high-stakes test. Giving students practice items is not the same as teaching them the content.

CHAPTER 2

These end-of-chapter quizzes are designed to get you talking with your colleagues. There are no right answers. When a school administrator like Mr. Clinton institutes a buildingwide initiative like this, he or she usually has decided that the way the teachers have been doing their job needs to be updated. In a case like this, the most open, mature, and collegial answer is *B*. Similarly, if you teach older students in an elementary building, you have a responsibility to advocate for their developmental needs. This includes asking the administration to consider option *D*, because baby work for older kids will get you nowhere. The teacher who answered *A* may be really frustrated with his or her job. Try to be supportive of district-wide school improvement initiatives until you have enough information to know how they are going to affect classroom practice. However, you may be in a building where the principal introduces a new initiative every semester. In that case, the best answer for you is to offer a gentle challenge to the principal in the form of *C*. If you answered *E*, you are not open to change. This might be because you are the only person in the building preserving best practice! In that case, the answer for you sadly just may be *F*.

CHAPTER 3

This is actually a true story. My student, Joe, tried every single one of these during the course of his exam. Joe couldn't get the Dragon software to work well, so he became frustrated. After a half hour of trying to get it to work, he asked for help in the office. The school secretary was happy to type for him, but Joe wasn't used to dictating his thoughts to a live person. As a result, after about half an hour, he became discouraged at the quality of the work he was providing. By the time I stuck my head in to the office to see how he was doing, Joe had asked the secretary to leave and was typing with his left hand. He was visibly angry. At that point, I told Joe to just stop and tell me in his own words what he thought the answers were to the items. It took a lot longer to test him orally, but it turned out he really knew his stuff. The incident made me think about UDL, Universal Design for Learning, and asking students to write essays to demonstrate social studies knowledge. The next year, I had choices for a final project that included a written essay, as well as other end-of-course products that would let students demonstrate their learning, such as an interactive map using PowerPoint or to using the flip phone to make a movie reenacting an event from our history lessons.

CHAPTER 4

Your school context is really going to affect how you handle this. Ideally, you should have an open relationship with your school administration, a relationship that allows for a conversation about the ways new initiatives are measured for efficacy. Some mix of *D* and *E* would be the best. If you decide that you are going to fully participate with this motivation program, in an effort to help your principal get the best data possible from this exercise, then your best answer is *C*. *B* is sort of a cop-out version of *C*. If you are going to participate, then go for it. The worst thing you can do is *A*, undermining the program before it even has a chance to get off the ground.

CHAPTER 5

What is the purpose of your book clubs? Hopefully, your main objective is to provide students opportunities to engage in real-life reading activities. Of course, all of us have had a few students who, for whatever reason, needed to be split up to get any work done. But if it is at all possible, some combination of *A* and *B* would be the best answer to this scenario. Read the book titles, give the book talks, and then let the students choose what group they want to be in using whatever criteria they want, just as adults do—and maybe the girls just want to be with their friends. I often read books that excited friends give me, even if I might not think I will like the book. Remember: the goal is to encourage a lifelong love for reading.

CHAPTER 6

I hope you answered *D*. Remember that best practice research tells us the best way to learn new vocabulary is to *read*.

Please refer to Chapter 9, where we list some other great tips for how to teach vocabulary.

Resource B

Five Ways to Teach Vocabulary

1. Read, read, read! Most vocabulary words are learned from context. The more words you're exposed to, the better vocabulary you will have.

2. Improve your context skills. Research shows that the vast majority of words are learned from context. To improve your context skills, pay close attention to how words are used. Get in the habit of looking up words you don't know. If you have a dictionary program on your computer, keep it open and handy. Use a thesaurus when you write to find the word that fits best.

3. Practice, practice, practice! Learning a word won't help very much if you promptly forget it. Research shows that it takes from ten to twenty repetitions to really make a word part of your vocabulary. It helps to write the word—both the definition and a sentence you make up using the word—on an index card that can be reviewed later. As soon as you learn a new word, start using it. Review your index cards periodically to see if you have forgotten any of your new words.

4. Make up as many associations and connections as possible. For example, the word BUFFOON can be made to look like a clown, which is a synonym:

BUFFOON

5. Play with words. Have word games in your classroom for your students to use in free time. Some favorites are Scrabble, Boggle, Apples to Apples, Balderdash, Bananagrams, word searches, and crossword puzzles.

General Glossary of Assessment Terms

Accommodation: A change in the way a test is administered to students with special needs. In general, students are assessed on the same tests and the same curriculum material as the rest of the students. An example of an accommodation would be to allow extra time on an unspeeded (untimed) test or a quiet place with few distractions to take a test.

Accountability: Being responsible for one's actions within an educational system.

Achievement test: An assessment that measures what students know and are able to do in a curricular area.

Alignment: When what is being taught is aligned with what is being tested. Alignment can be reported as a matter of the degree to which a curriculum's scope and sequence matches a testing program's evaluation measures. Similarly, alignment can refer to the degree to which a teacher's instruction matches the given curriculum.

Aptitude test: An assessment that measures a student's ability to learn or acquire a certain skill or ability.

Assessment: Any method or procedure used to gather information about behaviors. Qualitative assessments use verbal descriptions of behaviors while quantitative assessments yield numerical estimates, or measurements.

Assistive technology: A device or service that may be used by a person with a disability to perform specific tasks, improve functional capabilities, and become more independent.

Authentic assessment: Assessment of student learning within the context of real-life problems and situations.

AYP: Adequate yearly progress. AYP is a diagnostic tool that determines how schools need to improve and where financial resources should be allocated.

Best practice: Curriculum instruction and assessment that can be supported by quantitative and qualitative research.

Bias: When a difference in test scores can be attributed to demographic variables like gender, ethnicity, or socioeconomic status.

Competency test: An assessment that measures whether or not a student has the minimum skills and knowledge in—for example, a driver's test.

Criterion referenced: Scores are reported as skills mastery, either as pass or no pass, for a level of performance on a skills continuum. A score depends on a preestablished standard or criterion.

Cut scores: Also known as a passing score or passing point. A single point on a score continuum that differentiates between classifications along the continuum. The most common cut score, which many are familiar with, is a score that differentiates between the classifications of *pass* and *fail* on a professional or educational test.

Differentiated instruction: Providing students with different approaches to acquire new material regardless of level of ability.

Disaggregate: Test scores can be analyzed either aggregated (as a big group, such as a district) or disaggregated, broken down into smaller chunks called subgroups and special populations (such as race, ethnicity, free and reduced lunch, etc.). NCLB requires schools to compare the scores of certain populations of students against one another to examine achievement gaps.

Enacted curriculum: The content actually taught by teachers and studied by students. It might stand in contrast to the *intended curriculum*.

Epistemology: The study of the acquisition of knowledge, the social reproduction of selected knowledge, and the consequences of the acquisition and use of knowledge.

ESEA: An acronym for the Elementary Secondary Education Act 1965. Authorizes funds for professional development, instructional materials, resources to support educational programs, and parental involvement. The Act was originally authorized through 1970; however, the government has reauthorized the act every five years since its enactment. The current reauthorization of ESEA is the No Child Left Behind Act of 2001.

Face validity: Whether or not a test looks like it measures what it says it is measuring.

Formative assessment: Provides feedback about errors and misunderstandings of a lesson. Usually used by classroom teachers to make adjustments to teaching, to adapt lessons, and to individualize instruction.

Grade equivalent: A score that indicates the performance level of a student on a norm-referenced test in terms of grade level and month: for example, 3.5 (third grade, fifth month).

Growth model: A way of measuring student achievement goals by measuring students' progress from year to year.

Horizontal alignment: The degree to which an assessment matches the corresponding content standards for a subject area at a particular grade level.

Individualized education program (IEP): Students who receive special education and related services will have an IEP that is created by a team of teachers, administrators, parents, and often the student to make sure that the educational program is designed to meet the student's unique needs.

Intended curriculum: For K–12 education, the intended curriculum is captured most explicitly in state content standards—statements of what every student must know and be able to do by some specified point in time. It may stand in contrast with the *Enacted Curriculum*.

Interrater reliability: The extent to which two different people obtain the same result when using the same instrument to measure a student's achievement. Interrater reliability indices are expressed as a decimal from 0 to 1, with scores closest to 1 considered to be high.

Learning progressions: The sequence set of subskills a student will learn in a given unit of study.

Lexiles: A reliability score created by MetaMetrics, a company in North Carolina. Lexile scores often appear on score reports for high-stakes tests created for NCLB reporting purposes.

Modifications: A change to the curriculum when the goals or expectations are beyond the student's level of ability. The assessments for students with a modified curriculum will be fundamentally different from those of the rest of the class.

Multiple measures: Because no one test can ever tell you everything you would want to know about a student's knowledge, ability, or aptitude, educators use more than one piece of information to assess what a student knows and is able to do. Multiple measures include classroom assessments, portfolios, projects, and so on.

NAEP: An acronym for the National Assessment of Educational Progress (NAEP) is an assessment given to a nationally representative sample of school children in the United States to measure what students know and can do in mathematics, reading, and science for Grades 4, 8, and 12. The NAEP is created by the Institute for Educational Sciences (IES), a division of the U.S. Department of Education (created in 2002). The IES currently has contracted out the test development process to Educational Testing Service (ETS) in New Jersey.

No Child Left Behind (NCLB): An acronym for the legislation that was passed in 2001 in the United States that mandated that every state develop a set of standards for teaching math, reading, and science and have a system of assessment in place to measure student achievement and hold low-performing schools accountable for chronic poor performance.

Norm referenced: Compares examinee performance to the average performance of others in an identified reference group.

Performance assessment: Requires the demonstration of skill in applied, procedural, or open-ended settings. Performance assessments can be used to ask students to use knowledge from several areas to produce something.

Portfolio assessment: A collection of student work that reflects growth and breadth and includes student reflections.

Psychometrician: An expert in the theory and technique of educational and psychological measurement, which includes the measurement of knowledge, abilities, attitudes, and personality traits. A psychometrician holds expertise in the research and development of measurement instruments like questionnaires and tests.

Raw score: Score on an assessment before any statistical transformations have been made, such as the number correct.

Readability: A rough estimate of the reading skill required to read a text, usually presented as a grade level.

Reliability: The consistency of test scores on different items that cover the same skills or the consistency of an instrument by raters or observers.

Response to Intervention (RTI): An educational process that evaluates how well students respond to academic instruction, and then uses those student responses to guide educational decisions.

Scale score: Raw test scores are mapped onto a more meaningful and interpretable scale.

Standard setting: An official research study conducted by an organization that sponsors tests to determine a cut score for the test. To be legally defensible and meet the *Standards for Educational and Psychological Testing*, a cut score cannot be arbitrarily determined, it must be empirically justified. For example, the organization cannot merely decide that the cut score will be 70% correct. Instead, a study is conducted to determine what score best differentiates the classifications of examinees, such as competent vs. incompetent. Standard-setting studies are often performed using focus groups of five to fifteen subject matter experts that represent key stakeholders for the test. For example, in setting cut scores for educational testing, experts might be instructors familiar with the capabilities of the student population for the test.

Standardized: When tests are administered in a uniform manner in all schools. It is particularly important for the administrations to be standardized, if the scores from students are going to be compared against one another.

Standards: A body of subject matter content that is usually legally mandated and predetermined by a state department of education. Also conceptual or factual criteria representing knowledge, skills, or attitudes that are established by an authority.

Standards-based test: An assessment designed to measure student achievement in a content domain that is described by content standards.

Stanines: A 1 to 9 scale of percentages used to rank student performance on a standardized test to the performance of other students.

Summative assessment : A cumulative assessment that summarizes the accumulation of knowledge to that point. Can be used to grade student achievement in a course.

Think-aloud strategies: Students are asked to say out loud what they are thinking when they are reading so that the teacher can observe what is going on in the student's head when he or she reads. This can also be reversed, by the way, as a teaching strategy. Try to do a think aloud to model making meaning from a text with your students so they can see what skilled readers do.

Universal design for learning: An approach to designing assessments to make them accessible to the broadest spectrum of students. For example, a test might use only two colors to be sure that the design of the items does not inadvertently penalize students who are color blind.

Validity: The appropriateness, meaningfulness, and usefulness of the inferences that can be made from a test's scores. Validity in assessment refers to the extent to which test scores or responses measure the attributes they were intended to measure.

Vertical alignment: The alignment of different parts of an entire education system—from grade to grade—reflects the logical consistent order for teaching the content in a subject area.

References

Abedi, J. (2008). Classification system for English language learners: Issues and recommendations. *Educational Measurement: Issues and Practice, 27*(3), 17–31.

Afflerbach, P. (2007). *Understanding and using reading assessment K–12*. Newark, DE: International Reading Association.

Allington, R. L. (2001). *What really matters for struggling readers: Designing research-based programs*. New York, NY: Longman.

Allington, R. L. (2006). *What really matters for struggling readers: Designing research-based programs* (2nd ed.). Boston, MA: Pearson Education.

Ames, C. (1992). Classrooms: Goals, structures, and student motivation. *Journal of Educational Psychology, 84*(3), 261–271.

Anderson, R. C., Wilson, P. T., & Fielding, L. G. (1988). Growth in reading and how children spend their time outside of school. *Reading Research Quarterly, 23*(3), 285–303.

Atwell, N. (1998). *In the middle: New understanding about writing, reading, and Learning*. Portsmouth, NH: Boynton/Cook.

Baker, E. (2004). *Aligning curriculum, standards, and assessments: Fulfilling the promise of school reform*. University of California, Los Angeles: National Center for Research on Evaluation, Standards, and Student Testing.

Banks, J. (1996). The canon debate, knowledge construction, and multicultural education. In J. Banks (Ed.), *Multicultural education, transformative knowledge & action: Historical and contemporary perspectives,* (pp. 3–29). New York, NY: Teachers College Press.

Barrera, R. B., Liguori, O., & Salas, L. (1993). Ideas a literature can grow on: Key insights for enriching and expanding children's literature about the Mexican-American experience. In V. Harris (Ed.), *Teaching multicultural literature in Grades K–8* (pp. 37–53). Norwood, MA: Christopher-Gordon.

Beach, R. (1993). *A teachers' introduction to reader-response theories*. Urbana, IL: National Council of Teachers of English.

Bean, R. M., & Morewood, A. (2007). Best practices in professional development for improving literacy instruction. In L. B. Gambrell, L. M. Morrow, & M. Pressley (Eds.). *Best practices in literacy instruction* (3rd ed.), (pp. 373–394). New York, NY: Guilford Press.

Bhola, D., Impara, J., & Buckendahl, C. (2003). Aligning tests with states' content standards: Methods and issues. *Educational Measurement: Issues and Practice, 22*(3), 21–29.

Black, P., Harrison, C., Lee, C., Marshall, B., & Wiliam, D. (2003). *Assessment for learning: Putting it into practice*. Berkshire, England: Open University Press.

Black, P., Harrison, C., Lee, C., Marshall, B., & Wiliam, D. (2004). Working inside the black box: Assessment for learning in the classroom. *Phi Delta Kappan, 86*(1), 8–21.

Black, P., & Wiliam, D. (1998a). Assessment and classroom learning. *Assessment in Education, 5*(1), 7–74.

Black, P., & Wiliam, D. (1998b). Inside the black box: Raising standards through classroom assessment. *Phi Delta Kappan, 80*(2), 139–148.

Bloom, B. S., & Krathwohl, D. R. (1956). *Taxonomy of educational objectives: The classification of educational goals, by a committee of college and university examiners. Handbook 1: Cognitive domain*. New York, NY: Longman.

Bunting, E. (1991). *Fly away home*. (R. Himler Illustrator). Boston, MA: Houghton Mifflin.

Cai, M. (1998). Multiple definitions of multicultural literature: Is the debate really just "ivory tower" bickering? *The New Advocate, 11*(4), 311–324.

Cai, M., & Bishop, R. S. (1994). Multicultural literature for children: Towards a clarification of the concept. In A. H. Dyson & C. Genishi (Eds.), *The need for story: Cultural diversity in classroom and community* (pp. 57–71). Urbana, IL: National Council of Teachers of English.

Cameron, J., & Pierce, W. D. (1994). Reinforcement, reward, and intrinsic motivation: A meta-analysis. *Review of Educational Research, 64*(3), 363–423.

Cameron, J., Pierce, W. D., Banko, K. M., & Gear, A. (2005). Achievement-based rewards and intrinsic motivation: A test of cognitive mediators. *Journal of Educational Psychology, 97*(4), 641–655.

Chall, J. (1983). *Stages of reading development*. New York: Harcourt Brace.

Cipielewski, J., & Stanovich, K. (1992). Predicting growth in reading ability from children's exposure to print. *Journal of Experimental Child Psychology, 54*(1), 74–89.

Cizek, G. J., & Burg, S. S. (2006). *Addressing test anxiety in a high-stakes environment: Strategies for classrooms and schools*. Thousand Oaks, CA: Corwin.

Comber, B. (1999, November). *Critical literacies: Negotiating powerful and pleasurable curricula—How do we foster critical literacy through English language arts?* Paper presented at National Council of Teachers of English Annual Convention, Denver, CO.

Comber, B. (2001). Critical literacies and local action: Teacher knowledge and a "new" research agenda. In B. Comber & A. Simpson (Eds.), *Negotiating critical literacies in classrooms* (pp. 271–282). Mahwah, NJ: Lawrence Erlbaum.

Conlan, G. (1986). "Objective measures of writing ability." In Greenbert, K. L. and Slaughter, V. B. (Eds.), *Notes from the National Testing Network in writing*. New York: The City University of New York Instructional Resource Center.

Corcoran, B. (1992). Reader stance: From willed aesthetic to discursive construction. In J. Many & C. Cox (Eds.), *Reader stance and literary understanding*, (pp. 49–71). Norwood, NJ: Ablex.

Corcoran, B. (1994). Balancing reader response and cultural theory and practice. In B. Corcoran, M. Hayhoe, & G. Pradl (Eds.), *Knowledge in the making: Challenging the text in the classroom*, (pp. 3–23). Portsmouth, NH: Boynton/Cook.

Council of Chief State School Officers. (1999). *Student motivation: A statement of the Council of Chief State School Officers* from http://events.ccsso.org/content/pdfs/student_motivation.pdf

Creighton, D. (1997). Critical literacy in the elementary classroom. *Language Arts, 74*(6), 438–445.

Daniels, H. (2001). *Literature circles: Voice and choice in book clubs & reading groups* (2nd ed.). New York, NY: Stenhouse.

Deci, E. L., Koestner, R., & Ryan, R. M. (1999). A meta-analytic review of experiments examining the effects of extrinsic rewards on intrinsic motivation. *Psychological Bulletin, 125*(6), 627–668.

Donald, J. G. (1999). Motivation for higher-order learning. *New Directions for Teaching and Learning, 78*, 27–35.

Dr. Seuss (1999). *Hooray for diffendoofer day*. [Published posthumously by J. Prelutsky & L. Smith] New York, NY: Knopf.

Eco-Libris. (n.d.). Some facts about the book publishing industry. Retrieved from http://www.ecolibris.net/bookpublish.asp

Edelsky, C. (1999). Introduction. In C. Edelsky (Ed.), *Making justice our project: Teachers working toward critical whole language practice*, (pp. 1–6). Urbana, IL: National Council of Teachers of English Education.

Enciso, P. (1997). Negotiating the meaning of difference. In T. Rogers & A. Soter (Eds*.*), *Reading across cultures: Teaching literature in a diverse society*, (pp. 13–41). New York, NY: Columbia University Teachers College Press.

Fang, Z., Fu, D., & Lamme, L. (1999). Rethinking the role of multicultural literature in literacy instruction. *The New Advocate, 12*(3), 259–276.

Forsyth, R. A., Ansley, T. N., Feldt, L. S., & Alnot, S. D. (2001). Iowa tests of educational development. Itasca, IL: Riverside.

Fuhrken, C. (2009). *What every elementary teacher needs to know about reading tests from someone who has written them*. Portland, ME: Stenhouse.

Furst, E. J. (1963). The question of abuses in the use of aptitude and achievement tests. *Theory Into Practice, 2*(3), 199–204.

Gonzalez, V., Brusca-Vega, R., & Yawkey, T. (1996). *Assessment and instruction of culturally and linguistically diverse students with or at-risk of learning problems: From research to practice*. Boston, MA: Allyn & Bacon.

Good, R. H. III, Kaminski, R. A., Moats, L. C., Laimon, D., Smith, S., & Dill, S. (2002–2003). Test review of the DIBELS: Dynamic Indicators of Basic Early Literacy Skills (5th ed.). From R. A. Spies & B. S. Plake (Eds.), *The sixteenth mental measurements yearbook* [Electronic version]. Retrieved from the Buros Institute's *Test Reviews Online* website: http://www.unl.edu/buros

Goodman, K. (2006). A critical review of DIBELS. In K. S. Goodman (Ed.), *The truth about DIBELS: What it is, what it does*, (pp. 1–39). Portsmouth, NH: Heinemann.

Gottfried, A. E. (1990). Academic intrinsic motivation in young elementary school children. *Journal of Educational Psychology, 82*(3), 525–538.

Gross, M. (2000). *The conspiracy of ignorance: The failure of American public schools*. New York, NY: HarperCollins.

Guthrie, J. T. (2007). Reading motivation and reading comprehension growth in the later elementary years. *Contemporary Educational Psychology, 32*(3), 282–313.

Guthrie, J. T., & Wigfield, A. (2000). Engagement and motivation in reading. In M. L. Kamil, P. B. Mosenthal, P. D. Pearson, & R. Barr (Eds.), *Handbook of reading research* (Vol. 3), (pp. 403–422). Mahwah, NJ: Lawrence Erlbaum.

Hade, D. (1997). Reading multiculturally. In V. Harris (Ed.), *Using multiethnic literature in the K-8 classroom*, (pp. 233–256). Norwood, MA: Christopher-Gordon.

Harlen, W., & Crick, R. D. (2003). Testing and motivation for learning. *Assessment in Education: Principles, Policy & Practice, 10*(2), 169–207.

Harlen, W., & James, M. (1997). Assessment and learning: Differences and relationships between formative and summative assessment. *Assessment in Education: Principles, Policy & Practice, 4*(3), 365–379.

Harris, V. (1994). No invitations required to share multicultural literature. *Journal of Children's Literature, 20*(1), 9–13.

Harris, V. (1996). Continuing dilemmas, debates and delights in multicultural literature. *The New Advocate, 9*(2), 107–122.

Harste, J. (2000). Supporting critical conversations in classrooms. In K. M. Pierce (Ed.), *Adventuring with Books,* (pp. 507–554). Urbana, IL: NCTE.

Harvey, S., & Goudvis, A. (2000). *Strategies that work: Teaching comprehension to enhance understanding.* Portland, ME: Stenhouse.

Heritage, M. (2007). Formative assessment: What do teachers need to know and do? *Phi Delta Kappan, 89*(2), 140–145.

Hollingworth, L. (2007, December). Five ways to prepare for standardized tests without sacrificing best practice. *The Reading Teacher, 61*(4), 339–342.

Hollingworth, L., Dude, D. J., & Shepherd, J. (2010). Pizza parties, pep rallies, and practice tests: Strategies used by high school principals to raise percent proficient. *Leadership and Policy in Schools, 9*(4), 1–17.

Hoover, H. D., Dunbar, S. B., & Frisbie, D. A. (2001). Iowa tests of basic skills, forms A, B, and C. Itasca, IL: Riverside.

Hoover, H. D., Dunbar, S. B., Frisbie, D. A., Oberley, K. R., Ordman, V. L., Naylor, R. J., . . . Shannon, G.P. (2003). *The Iowa tests interpretive guide for teachers and counselors.* Itasca, IL: Riverside Publishing.

Horn, C. (2003). High-stakes testing and students: Stopping or perpetuating a cycle of failure? *Theory Into Practice, 42*(1), 30–41.

Hornof, M. (2008). Reading tests as a genre study. *The Reading Teacher, 62*(1), 69–73.

Hynds, S., & Appleman, D. (1997). Walking our talk: Between reader response and responsibility in the literature classroom. *English Education, 29,* 272–297.

Individuals With Disabilities Education Act (IDEA), 20 U.S.C. §§ 1400 to 1491 (1997). Retrieved from http://idea.ed.gov/

Jones, M., Jones, B., Hardin, B., Chapman, L., Yarbrough, T., & Davis, M. (1999). The impact of high-stakes testing on teachers and students in North Carolina. *Phi Delta Kappan, 81*(3), 199–203.

Kamii, C., & Manning, M. (2005). Dynamic Indicators of Basic Early Literacy Skills (DIBELS): A tool for evaluating student learning? *Journal of Research in Childhood Education, 20*(2), 75–90.

Ketter, J., & Pool, J. (2001). Exploring the impact of a high-stakes direct writing assessment in two high school classrooms. *Research in the Teaching of English, 35*(3), 344–393.

Kohn, A. (2000). *The case against standardized testing: Raising the scores, ruining the schools.* Portsmouth, CT: Heinemann.

Lasky, K. (1996). To Stingo with love: An author's perspective on writing outside one's own culture. *The New Advocate, 9*(1), 1–7.

Leland, C., & Harste, J. (2000). Critical literacy: Enlarging the space of the possible. *Primary Voices K–6, 9*(2). 3–7.

Lewis, C. (2000). Critical issues: Limits of identification: The personal, pleasurable, and critical in reader response. *Journal of Literacy Research, 32*(2), 253–266.

Lewison, M., Seely Flint, A., & Van Sluys, K. (2002). Taking on critical literacy: The journey of newcomers and novices. *Language Arts, 79*(5), 382–392.

Lindquist, E. F. (1970). The Iowa testing programs—A retrospective view. *Education, 81*(1), 7–23.

Locke, E. A., & Latham, G. P. (2002). Building a practically useful theory of goal setting and task motivation: A 35-year odyssey. *American Psychologist, 57*(9), 705–717.

Lohman, D. F., Korb, K., & Lakin, J. (2008). Identifying academically gifted English-language learners using nonverbal tests: A comparison of the Raven, NNAT, and CogAT. *Gifted Child Quarterly, 52*(4), 275–296. (Research Paper of the Year Award from the National Association of Gifted Children).

Luke, A. (1994). *The social construction of literacy in the primary school.* New York, NY: Macmillan.

Luke, A., & Freebody, P. (1997). Critical literacy and the question of normativity: An introduction. In S. Muspratt, A. Luke, & P. Freebody (Eds.), *Constructing critical literacies: Teaching and learning textual practice* (pp. 1–18). Cresskill, NJ: Hampton Press.

Luke, A., O'Brien, J., & Comber, B. (2001). Making community texts objects of study. In H. Fehring & P. Green (Eds.), *Critical literacy: A collection of articles from the Australian literacy educators' association,* (pp. 112–123). Newark, DE: International Reading Association.

Madaus, G., & Clarke, M. (2001). The adverse impact of high stakes testing on minority students: Evidence from 100 years of test data. In G. Orfield & M. Kornhaber (Eds.), *Raising standards or raising barriers: Inequality and high stakes testing in public education* (pp. 85–106). New York, NY: The Century Foundation.

Marshall, J. (2000). Research on response to literature. In M. L. Kamil, P. B. Mosenthal, P. David Pearson & R. Barr (Eds.), *Handbook of reading research* (Vol. 3, pp. 381–402). Mahwah, NJ: Lawrence Erlbaum.

Martínez-Roldán, C., & López-Robertson, J. (1999/2000). Initiating literature circles in a first-grade bilingual classroom. *The Reading Teacher, 53*(4), 270–281.

McGillis, R. (1997). Learning to read, reading to learn; or engaging in critical pedagogy. *Children's Literature Association Quarterly, 22*(3), 126–132.

Miller, S. (2002). Reflective teaching in the panic of high-stakes testing. *English Education, 34*(2), 164–168.

Morgan, W. (1997). *Critical literacy in the classroom: The art of the possible.* New York, NY: Routledge.

National Institute of Child Health and Human Development. (2000). *Report of the National Reading Panel. Teaching children to read: An evidence-based assessment of the scientific research literature on reading and its implications for reading instruction* (NIH Publication No. 00-4769). Washington, DC: Government Printing Office.

National Reading Panel. (2000). *Teaching children to read.* Retrieved from http://www.nationalreadingpanel.org./Publications/summary.htm

Nieto, S. (1992). *Affirming diversity: The sociopolitical context of multicultural education.* New York, NY: Longman.

Nodelman, P. (2003). *The pleasures of children's literature* (3rd ed.). Boston, MA: Pearson Education.

O'Neill, M. (1993). Teaching literature as cultural criticism. *English Quarterly, 25*(1), 19–25.

Paulsen, M. B., & Feldman, K. A. (1999). Student motivation and epistemological beliefs. *New Directions for Teaching and Learning, 78*, 17–25.

Peterson, J. J. (1983). *The Iowa testing programs: The first fifty years.* Iowa City: University of Iowa.

Piaget, J. (1972). Development and learning. In C. S. Lavattelly & F. Stendler (Eds.), *Reading in child behavior and development.* New York, NY: Harcourt Brace Janovich.

Popham, W. J. (2005). *Classroom assessment* (4th ed.). Boston, MA: Pearson Education.

Popham, W. J. (2008). *Transformative assessment.* Alexandria, VA: Association for Supervision and Curriculum Development.

Rhodes, R. L., Ochoa, S. H., & Ortiz, S. O. (2005). *Assessing culturally and linguistically diverse students.* New York, NY: Guilford Press.

Riordan, R. (2006). *The lightning thief (Percy Jackson and the Olympians, Book 1).* New York, NY: Miramax.

Roderick, M., & Engel, M. (2001). The grasshopper and the ant: Motivational responses of low-achieving students to high-stakes testing. *Educational Evaluation and Policy Analysis, 23*(3), 197–227.

Rosenblatt, L. (1982). The literary transaction: Evocation and response. *Theory Into Practice, 21*, 268–277.

Rosenblatt, L. (1995). *Literature as exploration* (5th ed.). New York, NY: Modern.

Rothman, R. (2003). *Imperfect matches: The alignment of standards and tests.* [Paper commissioned by the Committee on Test Design for K–12 Science Achievement]. Washington, DC: National Research Council, Center for Education.

Schunk, D. H., Pintrich, P. R., & Meece, J. L. (2008). *Motivation in education: Theory, research, and applications* (3rd ed.). Upper Saddle River, NJ: Pearson Education.

Soter, A. (1999). *Young adult literature and the new literary theories: Developing critical readers in middle school.* New York, NY: Teachers College Press.

Spinelli. J. (1996). *Crash.* New York, NY: Random House.

Standards for Educational and Psychological Testing. (1999). Washington, DC: American Educational Research Association.

Stiggins, R. J. (1999). Evaluating classroom assessment training in teacher education programs. *Educational Measurement: Issues and Practice, 18*(1), 23–27.

Stiggins, R. J. (2002). Assessment crisis: The absence of assessment FOR learning. *Phi Delta Kappan, 83*(10), 758–765.

Taxel, J. (1997). Multicultural literature and the politics of reaction. *Teachers College Record, 98*(3).

Thorndike, R.L., & Hagen, E. (1977/1955). *Measurement and evaluation in psychology and education.* (4th ed.). New York, NY: John Wiley.

Tomlinson, C. A., & Cunningham-Eidson, C. (2003). *Differentiation in practice: A resource guide for differentiating curriculum Grades 5–9.* Alexandria, VA: Association for Supervision and Curriculum Development.

U.S. Department of Education, the National Commission on Excellence in Education (1983). *A Nation at Risk: The Imperative for Educational Reform.* Washington, DC: Government Printing Office.

U.S. Department of Education. (2007). *Policy and program studies service report highlights: State and local implementation of the No Child Left Behind Act.* Retrieved from http://www.ed.gov/rschstat/eval/disadv/nclb-accountability/index.html

Valli, L., Croninger, R., Chambliss, M., Graeber, A., & Buese, D. (2008). *Test driven: High-stakes accountability in elementary schools.* New York, NY: Teachers College Press.

Vasquez, V. (2001). Constructing a critical curriculum with young children. In B. Comber & A. Simpson (Eds.), *Negotiating critical literacies in classrooms* (pp. 55–66). Mahwah, NJ: Lawrence Erlbaum.

Vasquez, V. (2003). *Getting beyond "I like the book": Creating space for critical literacy in K–6 classrooms.* Newark, DE: International Reading Association.

Verhoeven, L., & Snow, C. (Eds.). (2001). *Literacy and motivation: Reading engagement in individuals and groups.* Mahwah, NJ: Lawrence Erlbaum.

Vygotsky, L. S., (1978). *Mind in society: The development of higher psychological processes.* Cambridge, MA: Harvard University Press.

Webb, N. L. (1999). *Alignment of science and mathematics standards and assessments in four states.* Available from ERIC Document Service. (ED440852)

Webb, N. (2002). *Depth-of-knowledge levels for four content areas.* Available online at http://www.providenceschools.org/media/55488/depth%20of%20knowledge%20guide%20for%20all%20subject%20areas.pdf

Wolf, S., Ballentine, D., & Hill, L. (1999). The right to write: Preservice teachers' evolving understandings of authenticity and aesthetic heat in multicultural literature. *Research in the Teaching of English, 34*(1), 130–184.

Wollman-Bonilla, J. (1998). Outrageous viewpoints: Teachers' criteria for rejecting works of children's literature. *Language Arts, 75*(4), 287–295.

Yenika-Àgbaw, V. (1997). Taking children's literature seriously: Reading for pleasure and social change. *Language Arts, 74*(6), 446–453.

Index

CORWIN
A SAGE Company

The Corwin logo—a raven striding across an open book—represents the union of courage and learning. Corwin is committed to improving education for all learners by publishing books and other professional development resources for those serving the field of PreK–12 education. By providing practical, hands-on materials, Corwin continues to carry out the promise of its motto: **"Helping Educators Do Their Work Better."**